Y0-DYT-424

ISLAM IN EAST AFRICA

ISLAM IN EAST AFRICA

by

LYNDON P. HARRIES

UNIVERSITIES' MISSION TO CENTRAL AFRICA
35 Great Peter Street, London, S.W.1
1954

Made and Printed in Great Britain by
Parrett & Neves, Limited, Chatham
C6888

Contents

FOREWORD

I am very glad to write a foreword to this book by Dr. Lyndon Harries. Canon Dale, whom he mentions several times, was our expert in Islamics in Zanzibar, and it was in order to be an understudy to him that I myself first went to Africa in response to an appeal by Bishop Frank Weston. Dale could quote the Quran in Arabic with facility, and also the Muslim Traditions. He knew all the customary arguments in the Christian-Muslim controversy. The hope was that I should eventually be fitted to carry on this work in the approach to Islam on the intellectual and theological basis. But it was not to be. Within nine months of my arrival shortage of staff compelled the Bishop to send me to take charge of a parish, where the priest had fallen ill; then to another parish where the priest was leaving; after that to take charge of a boarding school during the headmaster's furlough; and finally, when the headmaster did not return, to remain in charge of the school with a good many other jobs added as time passed.

I have mentioned this for several reasons.

In the first place, what I saw of Dale's work and my own small efforts in the same direction led me to the conclusion that we shall make few converts from Islam through controversy on the intellectual level. Dale would have discussions with Muslim teachers, often surrounded by a large Muslim audience, and it seemed to me that he was quite first-rate in the way he presented his arguments and answered theirs. And they loved it, but they loved it as an argument. It was all perfectly good-tempered, and the Muslim audience seemed to applaud with equal pleasure when a debating point was made whether by Dale or their own leaders. One never seemed to get anywhere. As Dr. Harries says, the root trouble is that in Islam there is no sense of sin, as we understand it, and the exposition of a religion of salvation is meaningless until consciences have been aroused.

This does not mean that the intellectual approach is unimportant. When an educated Muslim has been 'pricked to the heart' and is beginning to feel the need of a Saviour, there must be someone who understands his theological difficulties and can help him to find his way through them. It is of great and urgent importance that there should be someone—better still a group of people—competent by hard study to deal with this side of the work. And, in spite of all staffing difficulties, it must somehow be made possible for them to have time for their study. This is my second point.

Thirdly I endorse all that Dr. Harries says about the importance of the witness of the African Church. The lives of African Christians, in whom the saving power of God's grace is manifest together with the joy which comes from a knowledge of His love, will do more than anything else to open the eyes and touch the hearts of Muslims. All the pastoral care bestowed upon African Christians is therefore a part—even the most important part—of the Church's task in the approach to Islam.

There are genuine Muslim enquirers, and there will be more as the Church in East Africa grows in grace. By 'genuine' I mean those who have become conscious of a sense of need, and do not merely wish to enjoy an argument. I hope Dr. Harries' book will help to secure the expert needed to deal with those who are proficient in their own Islamic theology. It will certainly help many non-specialists in their contacts with the ordinary African Muslims who understand little but assume a good deal. I hope also that many supporters of Christian missions to Muslim lands will gain from it a new understanding of the problem, and thereby a fresh incentive to prayer that the 'Reproach of Islam' may be rolled away.

G. W. BROOMFIELD.

INTRODUCTION

The great Samuel Johnson once said, "In the world of religion, Christianity and Mahometanism are worthy of attention; the rest are barbarous". With the knowledge subsequently gained about some of the other religions of the world, some would consider the term 'barbarous' as too harsh, but of course typically Johnsonian.

For our purpose it is sufficient to note that Dr. Johnson had a considerable respect for Islam. Christians generally have a respect for the Muslim religion, but without knowing very much about it. Books on Islam are many, but often they are difficult to read; they contain so many difficult Arabic words that the reader is discouraged. The religious system is usually described in such great detail that the reader loses his way in a labyrinth of unfamiliar description.

The present book, written for the Universities' Mission to Central Africa, is written with primary reference to that part of East Africa where the Mission is at work, Zanzibar, Pemba and the mainland opposite in Tanganyika. No attempt is made to provide a detailed survey of the past and present position of Islam in East Africa generally. The purpose is to help readers to understand something of the character of Islam in relation to the work of the Mission and to the African people. This does not involve a detailed description of Islamic belief and practice. The work of Canon Godfrey Dale, listed in the bibliography, may be consulted for further information on these matters, besides the many books written by other experts.

Islam presents a constant challenge to the Christian Mission in East Africa. The mere recognition of this fact is not sufficient. The challenge has to be met, but first it has to be more clearly understood.

9

Chapter One

THE MUSLIM COMMUNITIES

In East Africa, Muslims have for a very long time enjoyed considerable prestige. The most influential Muslim communities there are the Indian and the Arab-Swahili. The true Swahili people of the coast are the descendants of Arab merchants who married African women. Many of these families trace their origin back to Southern Arabia and the coastal regions of the Persian Gulf. Many of them maintain contact with their paternal homeland.

Some of the best-known Swahili poets of the last two hundred years belonged to high-born families in the Hadramaut, and the descendants in both countries can in some instances still be identified. The prestige of this Swahili aristocracy has been so high amongst the Bantu that many tribal Africans, with no Arabian connection whatever, have called themselves 'Swahilis' and become Muslims.

Besides the Indian and true Arab-Swahili communities, the Muslim population of East Africa consists of many tribal Africans living in villages on the mainland. Exactly how many there are it is impossible to say,[1] but in most of the rural areas where the Universities' Mission is at work, Islam is represented.

Of the Indian and Arab-Swahili communities near and along the coast, and, of course, in Zanzibar and Pemba, their background of Muslim culture and tradition, together

---

[1] In 1926 it was estimated at a million and a half *(The Call From the Moslem World)*, but is probably more than two million at the present time.

with their activities in the world of merchandise, accounts
for their comparatively privileged status in relation to the
majority of mainland Africans. It is well-known that the
Indians have for a long time played an important part in
the economic life of East Africa. Besides the wealthy few,
there are the countless shop-keepers in the towns and in the
small villages of the African bush.

*   *   *

It has not been possible seriously to attempt the conversion to Christianity of the influential Indian and Arab-
Swahili Muslim communities. The missionary's time has
been so fully occupied in shepherding and developing the
African Christian community, that he has had very little
time for direct and prolonged contacts with Indian and
Arab-Swahili Muslims.

The work of the Universities' Mission has from the first
been amongst Africans. The Mission has, of course, a
responsibility towards people of whatever race living within
its territorial boundaries, and whenever possible this
principle is put into practice. For instance, the influx of
many Europeans into the Masasi Diocese for the ill-fated
ground-nut scheme widened the pastoral responsibilities of
the Bishop and his staff, but there was never any doubt
that the Mission must undertake their pastoral care. The
work was an additional burden, gladly accepted, but additional to the main emphasis upon work for the Africans.

Similarly, a sprinkling of Indian Christians will be found
in most churches along the East African coast. They form a
very small minority of the Indian community; most Indians
are either Muslim or Hindu. Their new birth into
Christianity took place in India, in most cases within a

Christian community of long standing. They are by no means new converts, and, like many African Christians on the coast, are strangers away from their real home. For the missionary, his work is to shepherd these baptized people, whether they are Indians or Africans. This work leaves very little time for sustained and informed missionary work among Muslims.

In the early days of the Universities' Mission it was soon recognized that the conversion of Indian and Arab-Swahili Muslims was bound to be a long and very difficult task. Many of the first conversions to Christianity were of the redeemed African slaves. Arabs, engaged in slave-trading, were regarded by people in Britain, for obvious reasons, as enemies of the Christian Gospel. The influence of the Christian Church was exerted towards helping to put a stop to the slave-trade. It was considered that Islam and the slave-trade went hand in hand, so that to prevent the latter was to deal a heavy blow to the former. Much has been written on the subject by Christian writers which was not always fair to the Muslim slave-traders; the system of slavery as it was practised on the East African coast by Arab-Swahilis was not, in every instance, the heartless, brutal procedure it was generally believed to have been. But gross abuses of the system were common enough to justify its absolute censure by the Government and by the Church.

Later, whereas on the coast conversions amongst Muslims were practically *nil*, the Mission developed rapidly further inland amongst the tribal African communities. To-day, the missionary on the coast, living, say, in Tanga or Dar es Salaam, may be aware of his responsibilities towards the non-African Muslims, but, although he may have friends among the Indian and Arab Muslims, his effective work is done almost exclusively amongst Africans, shepherding the Christians who have come from up-country to work, and helping to build an African Church of believers whose traditional home is not any Islamic community, but tribal African society.

*   *   *

The most prosperous and best organized Muslim sect amongst the Indians is the unorthodox sect of the Ismaili Khojas, of whom there are something like fifty thousand in the Dioceses of Zanzibar and Masasi. If these people lived as a community on an island in the middle of the Indian Ocean, it would probably be considered the responsibility of the Christian Church to send missionaries for their conversion. Because in East Africa the Ismailis are a minority group, living side by side with Africans who are the missionary's first responsibility, they have been left without any direct religious challenge from the Christian Church. Friendly relations are maintained between the Mission and Indian Muslims generally, not least because no challenge has been directly offered by either side on the subject of religion.

The presence of the Christian Church in East Africa is, of course, to some degree a challenge to the religion of the non-African Muslims, but the fact that it is very largely an African Church does not promote their conversion. They naturally think—if they think about it at all—that the Christian missionary has come to serve, not themselves, but the Africans, and this is true enough in the circumstances. The non-African Muslims acknowledge the good work done by the Mission, especially in the fields of medicine and education. They know that the African is in need of much help. For their own sake they would be sorry to see the medical work curtailed; many Mission hospitals have a ward or houses for Indian patients. But any idea of considering the claims of Christ *for their own sake* is far from their minds.

* * *

The spread of Islamic faith and practice amongst Africans in East Africa has resulted chiefly from the influence of the Arab-Swahili, and not the Indian, community. In the mosques used by Indians, it is very unusual to find Africans praying side by side with them. This is not from any political or religious intention to keep Africans out of their mosques, but because even amongst their own countrymen the Indians may belong to an exclusive sect, separating its members even from Muslims of the same nationality. The Ithnasharis and the Bohoras are sects of this type. Amongst the Indians at least, there has hitherto been no common Islamic front to promote the Muslim religion amongst Africans.

A change in this respect may now be evident. It may not yet apply to the areas in which the Universities' Mission is at work, but what is happening in other parts of East Africa must have repercussions for the whole of the territory. For this reason it may be important to note that largely for political reasons some Indian Muslims are now occupying themselves as never before with considerations for the welfare of the whole African community. Whether such considerations will be put into effective practice remains to be seen, for up to now it is the Christian, not the Muslim, community which has promoted African interests.

At a conference of East African Islamic Associations, held in Nairobi in December, 1953, for instance, Indian Muslims declared themselves to be the champions of the

African cause. It was resolved that Muslim schools should be thrown open to African children. The whole emphasis of the conference was upon African interests. Phrases borrowed from Christian missionary usage were employed, for example, that Islam, as in the days of its first contacts with East Africa, would from henceforth pledge itself to "the sacred task of bringing light into the continent of darkness".

Nearly half of the two hundred delegates to the conference were Africans. Most of the speakers, however, were Indians. There can be little doubt that the purpose of the conference was political and only secondarily religious. It it well known that some nationalist Africans have been looking to India for support in establishing their political aspirations. The conference was an obvious attempt to win politically-minded Africans over to Islam. This political activity amongst Muslims is something quite new in East Africa. It does not reflect the spirit or the motives of the greater part of the Indian Islamic community there, but the conference has given at least the appearance of a progressive, united front claiming to represent the whole Islamic community. The strong proportion of African delegates to the conference does not represent the true relationship between them and the Indian delegates, for this relationship is deeply affected by differences of social and religious tradition even within the general Islamic community.

The religious differences within Islam between an Indian member, say, of the Ahmadiyya sect and an African Muslim of the orthodox Swahili tradition are at least as great as those between, say, a Seventh Day Adventist and a Roman Catholic. The further differences between a way of life deep-rooted in Indian social tradition and a way of life still linked with African tribal society widen the gap even more. The common brotherhood of Islam is a religious ideal, but in East Africa at least it is far from being an accomplished fact. If it were, there might be no need for conferences like the one just mentioned.

From the Christian point of view little can be gained by attributing to Islam in East Africa those advantages, like unity of purpose, complete inclusiveness, true brotherhood, which it does not actually possess. There has always been a tendency amongst Christian observers to speak or write about Islam in that country as though it were a consistent, orthodox religious system practised by Asians and Africans alike. This flattering conception has arisen largely because little attention has been paid to the sectarianism actually existing amongst Muslims. For the proper understanding of Islam in East Africa it is not enough to turn to the descriptive literature on orthodox Islam. It cannot be presumed that Muslims living in East Africa, whether African or not, live 'according to the Book', even when that book is the Quran.

*   *   *

Of the few Christian missionaries in East Africa who have made a serious attempt to understand the Muslim religion, Canon Godfrey Dale of Zanzibar was undoubtedly the most outstanding. The conversion of Muslims to Christianity was so important to him that he wrote books to explain Muslim belief and practice. Yet even he wrote of Islam chiefly in its orthodox form. His books provided a description of orthodox faith and practice, but he omitted to compare orthodox Islam with the forms of that religion which are actually found in East Africa. There can be little doubt that considerable numbers of Muslims in that country give as little assent to some of the matters described by Canon Dale as Christians are expected to do.

By presenting Islamic faith and practice as a consistent

whole, inconsistent only when contrasted with Christian doctrine or with inherent fallacies (from the Christian viewpoint) within the system, Canon Dale, quite unwittingly one must believe, was misleading his African readers into supposing that all Muslims believe and act alike. Very few tribal African Muslims are aware of the sectarianism within their own religion, but from the Christian point of view it is important that they should not remain unenlightened on the subject.

*   *   *

Sectarianism is more noticeable amongst Indian Muslims than amongst Arab-Swahili Muslims. The peculiar characteristics of Indian Islam in the mother-country, India, are not altogether absent in East Africa. Religious divisions are undoubtedly more numerous in India than in any other country of the Muslim world. It was Sir Shaikh Muhammad Iqbal, a leading Muslim philosopher of India, who summed up the situation in India not many years ago, a situation which, for the most part still holds good.

He asked: —[1]

"Is the organic unity of Islam intact in this land? Religious adventurers set up different sects and fraternities, ever quarrelling with one another; and there are castes and sub-castes like the Hindus! Surely we have out-Hindued the Hindu himself; we are suffering from a double-caste system—the religious caste system, sectarianism, and the social caste system, which we have either learned or inherited from the Hindus".

It is not suggested that Indian Islam in East Africa suffers so much from the double-caste system as does Islam

---

[1] *Indian Islam,* by Murray T. Titus, Oxford University Press, 1930, p. 171.

in the mother-country, but the system has to a certain degree influenced the practice of Islam by Indians along the East African coast.

Indian social religious life has not had the same influence upon African life as either the Arabian or the European. Africans have assimilated much from both the Arabian and the European worlds, but from the Indian there has been nothing like the same kind of interchange of ideas and custom. The reason for this may well lie in the persistence of caste-consciousness in the Indian community. This would strongly be denied by many Indians in East Africa, especially at this time, and, of course, it is not implied that Indians have regarded Africans as outcastes. But while caste-consciousness has had no legal or official sanction in recognized custom, its presence cannot be ruled out. Indeed, its presence is not confined to Indian communities in Africa, though one may observe more obvious signs of its effects amongst a community, like the Indian, in whose mother-country the caste system was a recognized, if regrettable, practice.

*　　　*　　　*

Islam, like Christianity, is a missionary religion, but the missionary as we know him has a more important place in East Africa amongst Christians than amongst Muslims. The unorthodox Ahmadiyya sect has a few Indian missionaries working amongst the Africans, but this method of promoting Islam is exceptional. Islam depends almost entirely for the spread of its faith upon the influence of the Muslim community. When social distinctions are overcome, the progress of conversion is likely to be accelerated. This is why the thrust from Southern Arabia and the Persian Gulf has resulted in the majority of conversions from paganism to Islam.

By marriage with the Bantu women, the Arab merchants were finding a home in East Africa not only for themselves, but for their religion as well. The true Swahilis are now a Bantu people, and the social gulf between the Arabs and the Bantu has been bridged. It is a bridge that many tribal Africans are attracted to cross. For them it leads, not only to Mecca, but to a companionship with fellow-believers of at least some common blood. The vast majority only succeed in getting a footing on the bridge. They do not go far along it, but it is far enough to make them content. They may not know what supports the bridge, but they ask no questions so long as they may be allowed to step back at will on their home ground. For that is where they still belong, to their traditional home of African tribal society.

Chapter Two

THE MUSLIM TRADITION

The Arab-Swahili aristocracy, like our own, has had to suffer some heavy blows to its pride. It is not what it used to be. Its former glory has sometimes been exaggerated by European writers. Hichens, for example, in a typical purple passage writes as follows[1]:

"By the dawn of the fourteenth century the fair citadels of Islam lay like a string of lustrous pearls along the green cushion of the verdant coast, their marts busy with merchants and seafarers and caravans trafficking in ivory, spices, gums, slaves, and gold from the Sofalan mines".

This is far-fetched, but the romantic description is based upon the indisputable fact that in the fourteenth century and for centuries before, there were coastal settlements, where the Arab-Swahilis enjoyed a standard of living far superior to that of any of the African tribes. Writing in the early 1500's, Duarte Barbosa related how in Pemba, Mafia and Zanzibar the 'kings' lived in great luxury and the people "are clad in very fine silk and cotton garments which they purchase at Mombasa from the Cambayan merchants. The women of these Moors (Arabs) go very bravely decked, they wear many jewels of fine Cofala gold, silver too in plenty, earrings, necklaces, bangles and bracelets and they go clad in good silk garments. They have many mosques and honour greatly the Coran of Mahamed".

The 'Cambaya' merchants to whom Barbosa refers were Indians from the port now known as Cambay on the gulf

[1] *Islam To-day*, by Arberry, article by Hichens, W., p. 119.

21

of that name north of Bombay. It is probable that even before the tenth century these merchants had established warehouses and had settled on the East African coast.

*   *   *

Enough is known about the very early history of the Swahilis to show, even at a modest estimate, that they enjoyed a prosperous existence with a high cultural background. Hichens is probably quite right in what he says about the Swahilis of the fourteenth century[1]: —

"By the wealth in his warehouse a man might be adjudged, but it was by the wealth in the storehouse of his mind, as a poet, a jurist, a theologian that he won that renown, respect and esteem which in these lands is called *heshima*. The early Arabian settlers had brought with them the art of writing, a marvel unknown elsewhere in Bantu Africa. They had brought with them too their traditional love of the arts of the poet and the bard".

The ruins of many mosques and mansions are testimony to the cultural values of Swahili life in very early times. The Kizimkazi mosque in Zanzibar, for example, which is famous for its beautiful floriated kufic inscriptions, was founded by Seyyid Abu Imran Musa bin Al-Hasan in the year A.D. 1107, and is a reminder of the high civilization and artistic culture of those early days.

This early civilization was thoroughly Muslim. There would now be further signs of the early strength of Islam on the East African coast if it had not been for the attempted destruction of Islam there during the sixteenth and seventeenth centuries by the Portuguese invaders. The Portuguese intended to destroy Islam, to secure the gold traffic of Sofala, to dominate the Indian Ocean and to

[1] ibid. p. 129.

banish all Muslims from its waters, to break the monopoly which the Islamic peoples held of the wealthy trade with India, and to divert it by way of the new Cape route into the coffers of Portugal. This was a 'Christian' war, to be compared, as to its spirit, with the Crusades, but it was a dark chapter, not only in Islamic, but in Christian history as well.

There is no space here for any details of the grim history of these two centuries. Hichens has written in this connection[1]:

"Mombasa was five times burned to the ground, its peoples put to the sword; yet it rose again and again from its smoking ashes and stands today with the scarlet banner of Islam flying from its battlements. Kilwa was ravaged with fire and sword . . . The mosques and mansions of Lamu and Pate were pulled to the ground or shattered by bombardment; sheikhs were put to death and the people were mulcted in huge fines for that they had done no more than defend their faith and the freedom of their native soil".

By the end of the seventeenth century the Portuguese invaders were finally driven from the whole coast north of Mozambique. The East African Muslims had appealed to the Imam of Oman, on the Persian Gulf, to help against their oppressors. This Imam, whose name was Ahmed bin Said, was the father of Seyyid Said, the first Sultan of Zanzibar.

*   *   *

It is salutary to note that from the two hundred years of violent domination by the Portuguese, no single mark or trace remained upon the faith or customs of the East African Muslims. All that remains of the Portuguese

[1] ibid. p. 122.

occupation are a few bush-grown ruins and, at Mombasa, that grim, shapeless mass of frowning rock, called, ironically enough, Fort Jesus. The two hundred years' war against Islam cannot be regarded as a victory for Him who said that 'all they that take the sword shall perish with the sword'.

In the eighteenth century there was a great resurgence of Islamic fervour throughout the East African coast. The merchant seafarers and coastal traders resumed again their ancient traffic with Oman, India, Persia and Arabia; and more, they turned their eyes to the promise of a new commerce with Europe.

A literary revival reflected the moods of the time. A spate of songs, poems, romances and epics marked the spirit of the liberation. Compositions like Seyyid Abdallah's *Al-Inkishafi* (The Soul's Awakening) were being read in the mosques throughout the coast. The minstrels' tourneys were revived, at which the people heard the latest compositions. Epics, known as *tendi* or *tenzi*, literally 'acts', or as we say, plays, became popular; among them were plays on the life of Christ, and the life of Job, as well as upon the life and death of Muhammad, and similar religious themes written by Muslims for Muslims.

By the end of the eighteenth century the outstanding Swahili poet, Muyaka bin Haji al-Ghassaniy, by trade a Mombasan shipper, had written poems on many different themes, both gay and serious, reflecting the substance of everyday affairs. This was the heyday of Swahili life, when the contrast between their own culture and that of the tribal Africans was clear-cut and unrivalled.

*   *   *

So it was when in 1832 Seyyid Said came from Oman with his court to Zanzibar permanently to reside there, but by that time rivals had appeared in the field. Pearce has written[1]:

"The Arabs who came from Oman with Seyyid Said were the pioneers of exploration in the Dark Continent, and the tales which they brought back of lakes and snow-clad mountains stimulated the interest of the Western world in Africa. Besides being merely traders, the Arabs settled in various parts of the interior, and, forming trading stations, became in time petty Sultans under the suzerainty of Zanzibar; and thus within a few years of his arrival at Zanzibar, Seyyid Said's dream of an African Empire stretching from ocean to ocean began to materialise. The whole African coast from Cape Delgado to Cape Guardafui acknowledged his dominion, and it seemed as if Zanzibar might really become the imperial capital of this African Empire.

"But Seyyid Said was born 500 years too late, for his aspirations and his ambitions of Empire were impossible of realisation in the nineteenth century, when European explorers and missionaries suddenly awoke to the fact that there was such a place as Africa, and that it was a continent worth possessing.

"So it came to pass that instead of allowing Seyyid Said to possess the land, the nations of Europe divided it among themselves.

"Seyyid Said was born out of due time!".

But Seyyid Said bore no ill will against the British. Britain, through the government of India, had already assisted him in military operations against rebels in Oman, and so he carried with him to Zanzibar a tradition of friendship with Great Britain which has endured, with even stronger bonds, ever since.

---

[1] Pearce, F. B., *Zanzibar, the Island Metropolis of Eastern Africa*, pp. 119-20.

During the first half of the nineteenth century the
political and economic centre for East Africa was
undoubtedly Zanzibar. Seyyid Said laid out the famous
clove plantations of the island. He stimulated trade and
commerce by a commercial treaty with Britain in 1839, and
he took the first step towards the abolition of the slave-
trade by his treaty with Britain in 1845, prohibiting the
export of slaves from his African dominions. He also
established commercial relations by treaty in 1833 with the
United States of America.

During this time the history of East Africa was centred
in Zanzibar and Mombasa. During the nineteenth century
the Arabs, represented by the head of the Muslim community, the Sultan of Zanzibar, were the only native people
of East Africa with consistent political importance. Apart
from their relations with the European powers, their
influence was great amongst the tribal Africans up-country.
There was an old saying:

    "When one pipes in Zanzibar,
    They dance on the Lakes".

But for the up-country native to-day, Zanzibar is no
longer the Mecca and the Paris of his imaginings; the Sultan
of Zanzibar is no longer for him his Lord of the World.
To-day they pipe in Nairobi or in Dar es Salaam, and to a
different tune. It is a tune with an European, not an
Arabian, setting. Times indeed have changed.

Chapter Three

THE CHALLENGE TO-DAY

The most popular tune in East Africa to-day belongs neither to the mosque nor the church, but to the political arena. It is being piped so loudly, and with such discordant notes, in Nairobi and elsewhere, that even in distant areas where Africans hitherto have not been much interested in politics, they listen attentively and with increasing concern. The religious music, whether from the mosque or from before the Christian altar, can scarcely be heard for the cacophonous din of political trumpets. Even so, for those whose ears are not already deafened by the political blasts, there is a preference for the Christian hymn over the Muslim chant. The preference is not always purely religious, though in some cases it is genuinely made. More often it arises from practical associations related to daily life.

The Christian hymn is related to the school and the hospital, to college and to individual status in a society with a predominantly Western trend. But, for the African, the Muslim chant has less and less relationship to the changing society in which he finds himself. There is still time for Islam to bridge the gap between religion and the facts of changing African life, especially if Islam should come out strongly on the side of African nationalism, but Christianity has had a flying start. The reason for this is that Christianity, and not Islam, is partly responsible for the changes which progressive Africans welcome in their traditional society.

*   *   *

If it be allowed—and this, of course, remains to be seen—the future of the African peoples lies very largely with those progressive Africans who identify themselves, to a large extent, with Western concepts and values. What has Islam to offer them? Up to now, very little indeed. Education after the western pattern has been provided by the Christian missions. While it may be possible for well-to-do Arabs to send their sons to British universities, Islam has not made the same provision for the sons of the poor African peasant. Yet they meet in our universities, because Christian missions have helped considerably to make the opportunity for the Africans. Indeed, the general standard of western education in many African communities where the Christian mission is at work is higher than in Muslim areas where the Christian mission is only represented.

The seed has been sown, and the parable of the Sower is being enacted on African soil. It *is* a Christian parable, and they were Christians, not Muslims, who sowed the seed. This is not just Christian propaganda. It is the Africans themselves who are living out the parable. We may observe at least some of the consequences of the sowing.

One thing is clear, that the sowing has directed the general trend of life and thought amongst Africans. The direction is towards the west and the Christian religion, and away from the east and Islam. For the time being at least, Islam in East Africa has lost its position as the directive for African hopes and aspirations.

There are obvious reasons for this—reasons which have little to do with the comparative merits of Christianity and Islam. Politics and economics can be either the friend or the enemy of religion, even though religion may not identify itself with either. At the present time, both politics and economics favour the development of Christianity in East Africa. The Christian Church is not responsible for this turn

of affairs, but it would be foolish not to take advantage of
it. This is precisely what the Church is trying hard to do.
In the very doing of it, both politics and economics seem at
times to be her most deadly enemy. This is the paradox.
But the general position to-day, with the majority of
Africans becoming aware of their own status in relation
to the western world, provides the Christian Church with
a golden opportunity.

*   *   *

Is it conceivable that the Church should lose this
opportunity? There is one great danger, of which the missionaries are aware. This comes from the very natural
association, in African minds, of the Christian religion with
forms of European government, or, indeed, with individual
Europeans. Africans used to believe that most Europeans
are faithful, practical Christians. They know better now.
Many of them realize that there are good and bad people in
every race. The vast majority of Africans may still have
no very pronounced views about the European Government
which controls their destiny. If they thought and understood
more about the aims of Government, they would be less
easily influenced by the emotional appeals of their political
leaders. We have seen in Kenya how suddenly and, for the
Europeans, how unexpectedly almost the whole of an
African tribe can be influenced for evil.

If ever it should appear that the legitimate aims of the
Africans are disregarded by the Europeans holding political and economic supremacy in East Africa, then the life
of the Christian Church there would be adversely affected.
The missionaries would teach what they teach now, that
the Church is not the Government, and some African
Christians would hold fast to that truth. But the vast

majority would turn inwards, away from the west, and look
for spiritual consolation elsewhere. It would certainly be
offered to them by Islam.

For the time being, of course, there is no question of any
grave diversity of aim between Church and Government.
Both are working for the welfare and betterment of the
African people. Nor is it suggested that Muslims are wait-
ing to take advantage of any future conflicts in the political
field. On the contrary, the Muslims of East Africa have a
long tradition of friendship with the British Government
and with the Christian missions. But no one can predict
with absolute certainty the future course of events in a
country where notoriously some of the best schemes of men
go astray. There is always the possibility that the pendulum
may swing once again towards Islam, which is an ever-
present factor in the general East African scene.

*   *   *

For Christians, there are two important conclusions to
be drawn from these considerations. The first is, that the
Christian Church must be made strong and independent of
political fluctuations. The Church in East Africa must be
free to express the mind of Christ even at the risk of losing
all political advantage. The absence of any such risk now is
no guarantee that it will always be so. Most missionaries
now in the U.M.C.A. areas are fully occupied with pastoral
duties amongst people who do not often talk politics to
them. Africans in those areas of East Africa, in Tanganyika
and Zanzibar, are not very politically-minded. But it would
be a mistake to think that even there the Church is being
built in a political vacuum.

The second conclusion is that Islam in East Africa is an
ever-present challenge to the Christian Church. Islam is

not in a hurry. Islam has survived ruder shocks in East Africa than the present loss of political supremacy.

Ever since Muhammad declared that Jesus was not crucified, Islam has been deeply committed to the spacious half-truth that divine favour is attended and evidenced by worldly success. Throughout the Middle Ages all appearances seemed to be in favour of that assumption, but when the tables were turned and the European nations proved more than a match for Muslim governments, there was no serious disintegration of Islam. There is a lesson here for East Africa. In other parts of the Muslim world a sense of inferiority has taken possession of Muslim peoples who have lost political prestige, but this has not affected their religious practice. If anything it has made them only extremely sensitive to the indignity—as they view it—of being proselytized, and there is certainly no sign of any large-scale turning away from the mosques.

Amongst East African Muslims any feeling of inferiority is offset by great pride in the past. This is very important, because amongst African peoples only a few can boast a known history going back several centuries. The history of most East African tribes is just a matter for speculation. To become a Muslim, then, means, for the tribal African, to share in a very ancient historical past, though it is doubtful if many actually get so far as to think of this. But the Arab-Swahili does, and he is proud of being different from other East African peoples in being able to look back so far into the past. So far as any sense of inferiority is concerned, Islam as a religion remains unaffected.

If anything, Islam is consolidating her position in East Africa. The challenge, then, belongs as much to the present as to the past or the future. The life of the Christian Church there may depend upon how that challenge is met. It cannot be ignored.

At the beginning of the present century Christian writers were asserting that Islam is nothing without political power, and that for this reason Islam in Africa could not survive. With this idea in mind, Atterbury wrote,[1] "Islam in Africa will be comparatively easy for Christianity to overcome".

No one can seriously believe this now. The challenge remains, and indeed is made more formidable because of the cross-currents of political feeling. In the long view there is always something to be gained by the religion which is not identified with political power, and it is because we know this to be true that we do not wish to see the Christian Church identified in fact or in imagination with any form of political government. Religion should be always on the side of Lazarus. Islam is in that position, generally speaking, in East Africa to-day. The Christian Church is trying to help both Lazarus and the rich man into Heaven, and is in a better position to influence the rich man than Islam is. Lazarus is being offered all that the Church has to give, and so long as Lazarus continues to understand this, he will rest on Jesus' bosom, and not on Muhammad's.

[1] Atterbury, Anson P., *Islam in Africa*, 1899, p. 183.

Chapter Four

ON BEING A MUSLIM

For the majority of tribal Africans, Islam has appeared as a support, and not as a challenge, to their traditional way of life. Within the framework of Islam it has been possible for the convert to retain the greater part of tribal custom without any radical change. In a true sense, no conversion is expected of the tribal African of East Africa in becoming a Muslim, for conversion means a turning away from those aspects of belief and of life which are not acceptable in the converting religion.

According to the orthodox Islamic view, polytheism, i.e. belief in the existence of more gods than One, is the only sin which is inconsistent with being a Muslim. This was never a matter of conflict amongst tribal Africans in East Africa. There was never a need amongst them, therefore, to turn away from any false belief in many gods, because in their tribal religion no such belief is to be found. They believed in one God, but without believing very much about Him except that He either created or called into existence the first living beings. The Makuas in the Masasi Diocese (Southern Tanganyika), for example, believed that God called out the first man, with his goats, from a cave in the Iluli hills of Portuguese East Africa, the traditional home of the Makua people.

Neither Islam nor Christianity has had to contend with false theological beliefs amongst pagan Africans in East Africa. Christian writers have previously remarked how God had not left Himself without witness amongst these people, and how traditional beliefs did not seriously clash with Christian doctrine. Their belief in one God, and in a world of spirits, has been regarded as a preparation for belief in Christian theology. The same might be said about preparation for belief in the God of Islam and in His angels.

The fact is that the tribal African, in East Africa at least, is no theologian, even though he is a very religious person. His belief in a world of spirits is not the same as a belief in a spiritual world. The spirits in the world beyond the grave are the fractious spirits of departed relations, who have to be placated and appeased by offerings of beer and beans. They dwell in no eternal city. There is no heavenly vision, but only an extension of village life after death. The world of spirits is not imagined as a place at all. Only the spirits are real, and they look down upon the life they have left with discontent at the way things are going without them.

There is no word for Heaven in the tribal languages of East Africa.[1] God has no Heaven in this pagan theology, and He Himself is undefined. He sends the rain and the harvest; He is Creator or Evoker. But of any personal relationship between God and created beings there is no trace. A relationship there may be between God and the tribe, for what theology there is is tribal, and God is the tribal God, not the Lord of the Universe.

* * *

Upon this mono-theistic foundation, either Christianity or Islam can be built. In the process the tribal African does not become a theologian, consciously choosing or

[1] The coined word in Swahili, for example, is *mbinguni*, which literally means 'in the clouds'.

rejecting beliefs from intellectual conviction. It is enough
for him to accept what teaching is offered to him, without
claiming to understand it all.

Every Christian missionary does his best to help converts
to as wide an understanding as possible of the central facts
of the Christian religion, but the long preparation for
Baptism is as much a time for testing the sincerity of moral
conversion as for instruction in the articles of Christian
belief. Only very rarely will a convert ask any questions
when being instructed, and the missionary sometimes thinks
that if questions *were* asked the convert would surely
understand the instruction better than often he does. In
other words, by the time of the Baptism, the convert usually
does know most of the Christian answers, but it is highly
doubtful if he has ever thought of any of the questions.

The same unquestioning acceptance by tribal Africans
is found in relation to Islam, with the important difference
that such an attitude is more easily identifiable with the
spirit of Islam than with the spirit of Christianity. A
Christian should be able to give a reason for the faith that
is in him. If reason does not supplement faith, there is
always the danger that those who are weak in faith may
fall away in a time of testing. This is especially true in the
Christian context, for faith in Christ involves the struggle
to bring all things to be obedient to His Will, and not, as
in the case of Islam, acceptance of all things as they are.

The very word Islam means 'submission' or 'resignation'
(to the will of God), and a Muslim is 'one who submits'.
Resignation to things as they are is a virtue in a Muslim,
and unquestioning acceptance, for better or worse, of God's
will is the ruling spirit of Islam. If the God of Islam willed
only what is good, then such submission could be equated
to the highest Christian virtue, but in Islam God wills all
things, both good and evil, even our very wills, and this

means unquestioning faith even in the rightness of what is bad for the souls and bodies of His created beings.

*   *   *

How then do men and women submit themselves readily to the will of such a God? The answer, of course, is that the theological formula of any Islamic doctrine does not exactly express a living reality in the thought and practice of any Muslim community. Professor Gibb of Oxford has written: [1]

"Muslim fatalism does not go very much beyond that found in any community (Muslim, Christian or Hindu) in which poverty and ignorance breed resignation in the face of bodily ills, physical disasters and the violence of tyrants. The ordinary Muslim takes thought for the morrow, like any other man: he assumes, like other civilised persons, that given actions will produce given results; and even in the matter of his future in the next life he takes predestination much more lightly than the Calvinist, since he believes that, whoever they may be whom God has predestined to hell fire, they are certainly not to be found in the orthodox Muslim community".

From this it will be clearly seen that Islamic doctrine, intelligently and fairly stated by authors of books on Islam, need not correspond with the actual faith of Muslims in any particular country. This is especially true of East Africa even amongst those who are orthodox Muslims. Orthodox Islamic doctrine is more properly a reference source with which the actual faith and practice of East African Muslims may be compared.

It would be easy to make an unfavourable comparison. Indeed, this has already been done by a Muslim leader of the Ahmadiyya sect, Sheikh Mubarak Ahmad Ahmadi. In

[1] Gibb, H. A. R., *Modern Trends in Islam*, p. 74.

the introduction to his recent translation of the Quran into Swahili he writes[1]: —

"Muslims (African) in this country (East Africa) are very poor specimens of what a true Muslim should be. The reason is that they do not understand the Quran. They may know how to read it, sometimes with a very fine voice, but how many of them know just what it is that God expects of them?". (Translated.)

The Christian missionary might feel grateful for this admission of inadequacy coming from a Muslim source, but the opinion expressed in the above statement is based upon an attitude quite unacceptable to orthodox Muslims, who form the large majority of Muslims in East Africa. This attitude implies a distinction between 'good' Muslims and 'bad' Muslims, but in orthodox Islam no such distinction is made. To an orthodox Muslim the words 'good' or 'bad', 'satisfactory' or 'unsatisfactory' as applied to a fellow-Muslim in respect to his religious belief and practice are inappropriate. There is only 'a Muslim' and 'a non-Muslim', only the believer and the unbeliever. To speak of nominal Muslims, in the sense that we refer to nominal Christians, is something that the orthodox Muslim never does, and it is important to note that the Sheikh Mubarak, who is quoted above, is a leader of an heretical sect.

The ideal of individual striving after holiness is, of course, not altogether absent from Islamic thought, but it does not have the same significance as in Christian tradition. In the Christian Church each member is called to be a better person than he knows himself to be. He is taught to obey the promptings of the Holy Spirit, so that by grace he may become more like his Master. But in Islam each member is taught to accept himself as he is,

[1] *Kurani Tukufu*, 1953, p. xviii.

for better or for worse, and if it be for worse, then nothing
can be done about it, since it is the will of God.

No special blame is attached to the 'poor specimens' who
do not understand the Quran. So long as they rehearse
their belief in the one God and in His prophet Muhammad,
they are true Muslims, and all else is God's will. There is
no doctrine of the Holy Spirit, no idea of grace, and therefore no emphasis on man's responsibility to respond to
those promptings which, in the Christian dispensation, can
reform and transform a man's life.

The Christian doctrine of the Holy Spirit is foreign both
to Islam and to pagan African society. In relation to the
Christian religion, therefore, there may be a great deal in
common between Islam and African tribalism as much in
matters which are not believed as in those which are. Belief
in the Holy Trinity and in the Death and Resurrection of
Christ are, of course, the most important.

*   *   *

But what are the positive Islamic doctrines which tribal
Africans can be said to believe with their understanding?
This is a difficult question to answer. A similar question
with regard to tribal African Christians, or even to many
European Christians, would be almost as difficult to answer.
In theory there are six articles of faith to which every
Muslim is expected to subscribe. It is probable that most
tribal African Muslims know something about them, but
not much. These articles have not been formulated into a
creed for public recital, but regular attendance at the
mosques cannot fail to familiarize African Muslims with
them. It is extremely likely that a great deal of prompting
would have to be exercised in order to remind some of the
faithful of them.

This does not mean that they are left without a creed to recite. Muhammad himself was not prepared to condense Islam either into a brief phrase or into a creed. As a result of controversies with heretical bodies or sects in the first century of the Islamic era, the doctors of religion condensed the discussions into summaries of the orthodox faith, but these summaries were not incorporated into public worship in the way in which the Apostles' Creed or the Nicene Creed are recited in the Christian liturgy. There is, however, the Recital of the Kalima, or Confession of Faith, also called *tashahhud,* from a root meaning 'to testify'.

*   *   *

The simplest form of the Confession is in the words, "I testify that there is no God but Allah, and Muhammad is the Apostle of Allah". A longer form consists of the words, "I testify that there is no God but Allah; I testify to His Unity and that He has no partner; I testify that Muhammad is His servant and His Apostle".

The recital of this Confession is the first of the five duties obligatory upon every Muslim. Usually in its shorter form it is uttered daily by every one of Islam's 350 million devotees. The recital of this phrase is what makes a person a Muslim. Certainly the daily and obligatory recital of this phrase, especially by an illiterate people, is a most useful instrument for maintaining a conscious sense of membership within the religion of Islam. A devout Muslim would not, of course, consider this to be its chief purpose.

The religious effect of the daily recital of this Confession of Faith cannot be over-emphasized. The phrase has been the battle-cry of Muslim armies everywhere. In days of peace it is a declaration, not only of religious faith, but of religious status. It is simple enough for an illiterate pagan

African to make it his own, without the need for theological enlargement.

The phrase is used individually by Muslims, but in practice it becomes more truly a slogan of group membership rather than a statement of intellectual and religious individual conviction. There are very few tribal African Muslims who adopt the same individual approach to their religion as Christians usually do to theirs. Whereas the African Christian is taught that he should be able to explain why he believes what he does, the African Muslim more often shifts the responsibility for doctrinal exposition upon his teacher. The group attitude in African Islam is reflected by the way in which responsibility for religious authority is passed on to an unidentified source. There is no argument, but only explicit belief that the theologians and jurists in Mombasa or Cairo or Mecca know all the answers, even if the individual African Muslim does not.

*   *   *

This attitude finds its counterpart in pagan African society. It is the avoidance of individual responsibility. A sense of individual responsibility is peculiarly a Christian concept, and is quite foreign to African tribal society. In tribal life responsibility, usually for what is bad, is shifted away from the individual either by the minute observance of the customary rites or by reference to magic. In the pagan initiation rites, for example, the careful observance of traditional custom by every person concerned, from the Chief down, has this purpose in view. Responsibility for what is favourable and good is shared by the tribe.

Such an attitude persists to-day, although it is affected noticeably by Christian influence even amongst those who âre not Christians. But it is there, and it lives on in the practice of Islam amongst tribal African Muslims.

*　　　*　　　*

It is not suggested that in Islam itself the individual is unimportant or that he is not expected to be individually responsible. Islam seeks the interests and welfare of individual men and women. But the general emphasis in Islam is much more upon the will of the people than upon the will of the individual. This is not surprising since acceptance of Islam implies submission of the individual will to whatever is decreed for it. Such submission certainly does not promote any form of individualism, but it does result in a very considerable spiritual strength in the people as a community.

Once again this corresponds to the strongly communal character of African pagan society. An African writer has said[1]:

"The God of the African was too remote to be concerned with the individual member of the clan".

The African has traditionally conceived himself as primarily a member of the group. This very fact has meant conflict wherever Christianity has come to African tribal society, for Christianity teaches the personal responsibility of the individual before God, and that the progress of society depends upon the acknowledgment by individuals of this responsibility, even when it brings them into conflict with the customs and conventions of existing society.

Conflict does not exist in anything like the same degree when Islam comes to African tribal society. Not the least important reason for this is that within Islam the African

[1] Mokitimi, 'African Religion', in *Handbook on Race Relations in South Africa*, 1949. p. 557.

retains his traditional psychological attitude of group dependence. He is able to do this without renouncing much in his
tribal life which as a Christian individual he must renounce.
The Christian community cannot exist within an unchanged
tribal community. In the most important respects, the
Muslim community can.

*   *   *

While these factors may help to explain why Islam, without the superstructure of schools and hospitals provided
by the Christian Church, has been widely accepted in rural
Africa, such considerations may be thought to be increasingly irrelevant because tribal society is changing in any
case. The breakdown of tribal sanctions, and therefore of
group dependence, is not equally consistent in all areas,
but it cannot be denied that western economy and concepts
have penetrated everywhere in East Africa. This may be
interpreted to mean that many Africans, whether they like
it or not, are being forced by the course of events to become
individually responsible for their own welfare in a society
more closely approaching that of western civilization.

The question then is whether Islam can maintain itself
within an African society which is strongly influenced by
western concepts of individualism and free will. To give a
negative answer is easy enough, but, of course, the question
itself is suspect, for it implies the complete dominance of
western ideals in African society, and this is contrary to the
facts even in those areas of Africa most strongly influenced
by western civilization. Even in centres like Nairobi or
Johannesburg, the persistence of traditional attitudes from
tribal life is a remarkable proof of the conservatism of
African ways of life.

Tanganyika and Zanzibar are less affected by western

economic change than many other African areas, but even
if this were not so, it would be over-optimistic to suppose
that further changes in the direction of western civilization
would adversely affect the position of Islam. The Christian
Church rightly claims that with the breakdown of tribal
life, the Christian religion puts something of the greatest
value in its place, namely, a religion in which the individual
can find his highest fulfilment. The Muslim would certainly
make the same claim for his own religion, for Islam has its
place also in the modern world. But for the time being in
East Africa, the claim is not really applicable, because tribal
life and the attitudes traditionally belonging to it are still
very much alive.

The number of Africans who have become completely
westernized is very small indeed, and even of them it is
doubtful if the word 'completely' is the right word to be
used. Many of them would resent its use in relation to themselves, because they are proud of their African background,
and such pride implies more than perhaps they themselves
realize. It implies that they have not gone over 'completely'
to the western camp.

If this be true of the most advanced Africans, how much
more must it be true of their more conservative brethren.
Only a few Muslim Africans have reached university level,
and most of these belong to Arab-Swahili families, and not
to traditional tribal society in East Africa. The vast majority
of African Muslims are, like most African Christians, still
living in a society in which tribalism exercises a powerful
influence, if not still in practice, then in traditional attitudes
of mind. In the event of a complete divorce from practical
tribalism, these attitudes will persist. The attitude of group
dependence can survive in Islam when the tribal society is
no more. Only a change of group-allegiance is involved,
and not a change in traditional outlook.

At present, and in spite of all that may have been written to the contrary, the Christian Church has the harder task of teaching the personal responsibility of the individual before God. However much we may speculate about future change in Africa, this will remain the most difficult task for the African to-day however progressive or backward he may be.

Chapter Five

MUSLIM BELIEF

If it be accepted that individualism amongst Africans will increase—and the present writer accepts this only with the reservations already made—then it will be necessary for the individual Muslim to look more closely at the articles of his belief. A brief reference can now be made to the six articles of Muslim belief, bearing in mind that they are not formulated in a creed of public recital, but that an instructed Muslim is expected to know and believe in them.

1. Belief in God

This is expressed in the short and trenchant phrase, *La ilaha illa Allah:* There is no god but Allah. The first word *la* is a negation and rules out any other god. Indeed, it rules out any speculation about Allah as well. Ask a Muslim who or what is God, and he is likely to reply, "Anything that you may think about God, be assured that He is not that". In other words, any statement made about God by mortal and finite man, by definition God is not that. He is the living one, having neither associate nor equal; He is neither begotten nor does He beget; He is omniscient and omnipotent; He wills all things, good and evil; He sees all things, even 'the steps of a black ant upon a black stone on a black night'.

The rosary, carried by some pious Muslims, contains ninety-nine beads or thirds thereof, and is meant as an aid in enumerating the ninty-nine 'beautiful names' or attributes of God. Most of these names occur in the Quran, and one of them is *al-Wadud*, 'the loving', a name which is used very frequently in Swahili religious poems written in the Arabic script. Nearly all of these poems, if they are of any length, begin with the words: 'In the Name of God the Compassionate the Merciful'.

Most of the ninety-nine names of God are the 'terrible names', emphasizing absolute power and sovereignty. While it is undoubtedly true that the Muslim conception of God is of an unconditioned, irresponsible Absolute, there is something to be said for the Swahili preference for dwelling upon the merciful nature of the Deity. They are a gentle, courteous people, a fact which has sometimes been attributed to the influence of Islam upon their way of life. But if conduct should correspond with doctrine, one might expect a different emphasis in their manner of life, arbitrary and aggressive. It cannot be taken for granted that the gentler side of Swahili life is the direct result of religious influence, though even Christian writers have associated the two. It may well be that the Swahilis of the coast, with their admixture of Bantu and Arab stock, retain inherent mental attitudes, different from those of the pure Arab, and that it is their religion, and not their own temperament and character, which is influenced by their outlook.

Every Sura or Chapter of the Quran, except one, is introduced by the same phrase employed in Swahili religious verse, referring to the Merciful God. This is one of the first phrases in Arabic, perhaps the very first, learned by the beginner in his introduction to the language, and for the tribal African Muslim as well may have more lasting effect upon his understanding than anything else he may subsequently learn about the nature of God. The vast majority do not get much further than the first steps in the Quran and in Arabic. There is very little use, therefore, in emphasizing the 'terrible names' of God in relation to these believers. While the emphasis must be taken into account in any consideration of Islamic doctrines, it may have little relevance to the belief of what we might call the elementary Muslims.

*   *   *

2. . . . . and in His angels.

Of these, the archangels are: Gabriel, who conveys the divine word to prophets; Michael, who provides all creatures with sustenance; Azrael, the angel of death, who receives the souls of the departed; and Azrafel, the angel of the resurrection, who will usher in that day with the blast of the trumpet. The last two are not mentioned in the Quran by name.

Angels are free from sin, they intercede for men, and also act as guardians. Eight angels support the throne of Allah, nineteen have charge of hell. Two black angels with blue eyes, called Munkar and Nakir, interrogate the soul immediately upon burial. If the answer is, 'Allah is my Lord, Islam is my religion, Muhammad is my prophet', the soul is permitted to enter heaven.

Although much of this angelology has been borrowed from Judaism and Christianity, there are important differences, e.g. in Islam angels are commonly regarded as of lower rank than the prophets, and they cannot protect a man from his assigned destiny. There are many other beliefs concerning angels in Islam which are peculiar to that religion, e.g. that the angels were bidden by God to do obeisance to Adam, that Shaitan (Shetani, or Satan) refused and was cast into hell; but any detailed account of Islamic belief in angels would be irrelevant for our purpose. Amongst the coastal Muslims there is considerable knowledge of angelology, but with tribal African Muslims the related belief in jinns (genii) is of more practical consequence. The Quran is definitely committed to a belief in jinns, creatures midway between angels and men, created from fire several thousands of years before the creation of mankind. Modern Indian Muslims try to interpret this belief metaphorically, but tribal African Muslims accept the Quran literally in this respect. They believe in jinns and fear them; they wear charms containing extracts from the Quran as a protection against them. Indeed, they know the jinn in their traditional pagan life.

Amongst the Makonde in Southern Tanganyika, for instance, there is a widespread belief in a jinn called Nandenga. No one will confess that he has actually seen Nandenga, but they all know what he looks like. He is very small, but with a long beard, rather like one of Snow White's seven dwarfs, but without their unfailing benevolence. He is autocratic and his commands must be obeyed. The people have been known to refuse to plant an important crop, like ground nuts, in a given year, because Nandenga had forbidden them to do so. This astonishing group-behaviour, based upon superstition, indicates the powerful hold of traditional belief upon everyday affairs. The whole child-population of a village may appear with a patch of hair shaven, because, the parents maintain, Nandenga has ordered it, and if he is not obeyed, harm will befall the village.

To find in the Quran justification for their pagan belief in jinns is, for them, evidence of the truth of Islam in contrast with Christianity which denies the existence even of Nandenga! One point of comparison like this is enough to bind the people to Islam in spite of all the enlightened reasoning that can be brought to expose the fallacy of their belief.

*   *   *

3. . . . . and in His books.

Allah revealed 104 books to prophets including the following: Adam ten, Seth fifty, Enoch thirty, Abraham ten,
all of which are lost. To Moses was revealed one book, the
Pentateuch; to David one, the Psalms, to Jesus one, the
Gospel, and to Muhammad one, the Quran. It is believed
that the Quran contains the compendium or gist of all the
others and is the all-sufficient revelation which cannot be
abrogated or superseded. Where the Bible contradicts the
Quran it is said to have been corrupted by Jews or
Christians.

It is obvious that the Gospels, with their accounts of the
crucifixion of our Lord, cannot have been corrupted with
the express purpose of denying the assertion of the Quran
that He was not crucified, since there are manuscripts, e.g.
the Vaticanus and Sinaiticus, which were written centuries
before Muhammad was born. The more enlightened
Muslim does not press this charge of textual corruption,
but adopts some other argument, like the one that Jesus
took the true Gospel with Him when He ascended into
Heaven, and that the extant Gospels are therefore not true.
But whatever theory is adopted, even the claim that the
Quran abrogates all preceding scriptures, the problem for
the Muslim remains by the fact that according to the New
Testament Jesus was crucified, and according to the Quran
He was not.

All Muslims believe that Allah revealed Himself in the
Quran. Muhammad did not compose the book; he was the
passive instrument repeating what he was told. At various
times and under varying circumstances over a period of
twenty-three years Allah, through Gabriel, spoke to His
prophet at whose dictation the messages were transcribed
on ribs of palm trees, tablets of white stone, and shoulder-
blades of sheep, or enshrined in the memories of men. To

the pious Muslim the Quran is, therefore, Allah's Book, not to be touched with unwashed hands, nor ever to be held below the waistline. Every letter is sacred and the book in letter and meaning is divinely inspired.

There are one hundred and fourteen chapters in the Quran, some as short as the Lord's Prayer, and some as long as the Book of Genesis. The chapters are named, not numbered, as, for example, 'Daybreak', 'Abundance', 'Women', chiefly because of the occurrence of these words in that particular chapter. The first chapter, 'El Fatiha', is said daily and many times a day in every prayer and is, in general, the equivalent of the Lord's Prayer among Christians. This is the English translation by Rodwell:

El Fatiha

In the Name of God, the Compassionate, the Merciful,
Praise be to God, Lord of the Worlds,
The compassionate, the merciful.
King on the day of reckoning.
Thee only do we worship, and to Thee do we cry for help.
Guide Thou us on the straight path,
The path of those to whom Thou hast been gracious,
With whom Thou art not angry, and who go not astray.

The language of the Quran is in general a rhymed prose, stately and sonorous, with a cadence which is entirely lost in translation. The Quran is essentially untranslatable and certainly in translation is a tedious book to read. Even an enthusiast like Carlyle said it was "as toilsome reading as I ever undertook. A wearisome, confused jumble . . . endless iterations, long-windedness . . . Nothing but a sense of duty could carry any European through the Quran". But the Muslim enthusiastically proclaims it as the sum of all literary perfections, and the more conclu-

sively to demonstrate its divine origin he insists that
Muhammad could neither read nor write.

*　　　*　　　*

The orthodox Muslim has a repugnance to translations
of the Quran, because he believes the words to be the
ipsissima verba, the very words, of God. Even if he does
not understand Arabic, he will read it to acquire merit.
Canon Dale translated the Quran into Swahili in 1923 in
the hope that Muslims might study the text intelligently
and, perhaps, critically. His translation displeased the
coastal Muslims, few of whom bought a copy or read it;
but the work had a wide sale amongst tribal African Muslims, not because they approved the translation, but because
this was just another book in a comparatively bookless
land. It is doubtful if the majority even knew that translations of the Quran are traditionally frowned upon by the
orthodox. Many of those who bought the translation were,
in any case, like Muhammad himself in that they could
neither read nor write.

Canon Dale had in mind Christian teachers living in
Muslim districts. For them it was important that they
should know what the Quran is about, and indeed most of
what Dale wrote in his other books helped Christians more
than Muslims to understand Islam. In practice, however,
much of the knowledge thus acquired remained only an
academic exercise, for without some intellectual response
from the Muslims the African Christian teacher, in his
effort to present the comparative merits of his own religion
and Islam, was ineffectually beating the air.

Islam in East Africa twenty years ago made little appeal
to the intellect, so that any use of the intellect in combating
Islam was bound to be profitless. To-day the position is not
quite the same, though most tribal African Muslims are

not able to make for themselves, even if they wanted to, a
mindful comparison of the two religions. But Muslims
themselves, at least the more progressive and therefore the
less orthodox of them, are employing methods of promoting
Islam which call for the use of the intellect by those
Africans for whom such efforts are undertaken.

A new translation of the Quran appeared in 1953, published in Nairobi, and written by Sheikh Mubarak Ahmad
Ahmadi, a leader of the Ahmadiyya sect. This Swahili
translation contains a commentary on the Quranic verses
written from the Ahmadiyya view-point, and combines
the presentation of Ahmadiyya teaching with continual tilt-
ing at Western critics of the Quran, especially Canon Dale.
The work is modelled on the English translation and commentary by an earlier Ahmadi, the Sadar Anjuman Ahmadiyya, of Pakistan, but is brought up to date by references
to recent translations of the Bible, especially the Union
Version of the Bible in Swahili, and to comments in the
modern East African press and by leaders like the Arch-
bishop of York.

This book presents a great show of learning and
modernity, but it is clearly bogus, not only from the
Christian but also from the orthodox Islamic view-point.
It is clearly meant for the African intelligentsia, but it is
doubtful if they will be interested in following the trans-
lator through the complex labyrinth of theological argument. Besides, the work has not political appeal even
though it maintains the traditional concept of the theoretical equality of all Muslims. Orthodox Muslims reject the
translation, and it is too expensive for the ordinary African
to buy. The chief interest in the work is the implicit recognition of the fact that in modern Africa Islam must take
into account the growing number of Africans who, as we
say, have a mind of their own.

The real problem, however, both for Islam and for the Christian Church, is that African minds are preoccupied with secular education. It is the 'educated man', the man with a degree who earns good money, not the religious leader or prophet, who is emulated to-day.

* * *

The passion for secular education along western lines is beginning to be shared by Muslims and Christians alike. Formerly only the Christians sent their children to mission schools, and at first even they had to be persuaded to do so. But now the passion for western education is widespread. Muslims prefer to send their children to government schools for obvious religious reasons, but in the up-country districts such schools are very few and far between. The greater part of western education is provided by the Christian missions.

There are no Muslim schools promoted solely by Muslims corresponding in method and scope to the Mission schools. The only form of education provided for African Muslim children by Islam is that of the Quranic schools. This does not involve a school building. The children sit under the eaves of the Muslim teacher's house, and are taught to read the Quran in Arabic. They repeat verses from the Quran. There is no general education of any kind; the teacher's job is to help the children to become good Muslims. It is religious education of a sort and no doubt, in spite of the difficulties of introducing children from tribal African society to Islamic religious practice, it is generally effective. But the purpose and the achievement is limited; so limited, in fact, that Muslims are increasingly aware of how far their own children are being left behind on the educational ladder.

On the coast the best government-sponsored Muslim schools can compare quite favourably with the best Mission schools. They provide for the Indian and Arab children. There is a new drive, however, in secular education to-day on the coast, and the Ismaili Khojas have been chiefly responsible for the building of nearly fifty new schools, including three secondary schools, since the second World War. The idea that Islam is inevitably divorced from educational progress in the western sense, and for Africans, can no longer be maintained. It is reasonable enough to suppose, however, that the present emphasis, chiefly by Indian Muslims, upon secular education for Africans as well as for Indians and Arabs, springs from secular, not religious, motives. The Christian Church was ready to give the African the very best education the Church could provide even when the African was politically unimportant. The reason for this was and still is a religious one. Islam was not equally ready.

*   *   *

Only to-day, when the African is achieving his own place in world society, is Islam recognizing in practice that for African Muslims the Quran by itself is not enough. If it be maintained that secular education of the African is eventually the responsibility of Government, and not of any religion, Islam in East Africa has still to reckon with the fact that it was the Christian Church which took the lead in African education. Thoughtful Africans will, it is hoped, always remember this. The spread of secular education, sponsored by Government, is inevitable in East Africa, as in other parts of the African continent, but for the Africans the foundation has been laid by the Christian missions and not by Islam.

Neither religion wishes African education to become completely secular, and the Christian missions will keep their own schools for as long as is possible. The greatest spiritual danger for the African is already only too obvious, namely, materialism. The Bible teaches men how best to face this danger. The Christian Church to-day is not identified with the obvious materialism of the west, and is opposed to it. The Church in Africa has always been led by men who from love of Christ have turned their backs on material or personal advantage. The missionary in his simple home in the African bush is most emphatically not, as some people like to think of him, a relic of British imperialism, but more truly a living example of the Faith which overcomes the world and of the life in Christ.

*   *   *

But what does the Quran teach to help men against materialism? Many texts in the Quran say that God moves man as He wills and as many more assert that man is his own master. There is no clear standard of conduct. The body of literature called the Traditions resulted from the very inadequacy of the Quran as a guide for living. There grew up a record of all that Muhammad was reported to have said and done, from which is also deduced what he might and might not have said and done or allowed. The Traditions are second only to the Quran in authority. It is recorded of Ibn Hanbal, one of the four great doctors of the law, that he would not eat water-melons because he could not discover how the Prophet ate them, an attitude illustrating the exaggerated reverence which Muslims pay to the minutest particulars regarding the Prophet.

In the Quran itself man is awakened to a higher consciousness of his relation to God and the universe, but

because of the separateness of God from the world
("nothing is like Him") and of the absence of any consistent teaching about the nature of man, there is no clear
direction as to man's conduct for the whole of life in human
society. This vagueness is not adjusted in the Traditions.

So long as the mass of the people are content to go on as
they are, accepting the Quran without question and praying
in the orthodox manner, materialism presents no great hin-
drance to the religion of Islam. As one writer has euphemi-
stically expressed it,[1] "Islam does justice to both worlds, the
here and the hereafter". But when western ideas arouse an
element of self-criticism within Islam itself, modern Muslims are forced to consider more closely the relevance of
the Quran to the world in which both we and they live.
Professor Tritton, who has spent his life in the study of
Islam and of the Arabic language, has written as follows
of the efforts of the modernists to interpret their religion
anew:[2]

"The problems facing the modernist are economic, social
and religious: he knows that something ought to be done
but he does not know what. . . . . The modernists have
not been able or have not tried to question the authority
of the Koran as the word of God but accept it as the foundation of their religion. They have interpreted it to mean
the opposite of what it says, have read into it meanings that
would have astonished Muhammad if he could have understood them but, in so doing, they have followed vaguely
liberal ideas and have had no consistent philosophy to guide
them. Their method was entirely subjective. Any attempts
to form a critical estimate of the Koran have faded away
and no one hints that there is in it a human element which
has to be judged like other things human".

---

[1] Tritton, A. S. in *Islam*, 1951.
[2] Tritton, ibid. pp. 169-170.

As in other countries, Islam in East Africa has felt the influence of Christianity, and coastal Muslims, especially the Indians, feel an urge to prove that Islam is in no way inferior in its doctrines, morals and social results. But what they claim for Islam is not visible in its East African history, nor for that matter in its world history. This does not prevent them from affirming, as moderate progressive Muslims do elsewhere in the modern world, that Islam, if interpreted according to their principles, will provide the only solution for modern social, political and religious problems. The brotherhood of men in Islam, a theoretical equality which is not the same as political democracy, is emphasized, and Muslims have been heard to speak of God as their Father, though the Quran describes this as blasphemy. Muhammad himself borrowed from the Bible, and Muslims to-day, consciously or not, borrow much from Christian ideology even in matters which the Quran does not support.

* * *

4. . . . . and in His prophets.

In Islam an Apostle (*rasul*) ranks higher than a Prophet (*nabi'*), for an apostle is not only inspired like a prophet, but has a special mission entrusted to him. Every apostle is a prophet, but not every prophet is an apostle. *Rasul* is the word used of Muhammad in the Recital of the Kalima. Eight apostles are mentioned in the Quran, but the twelve apostles of the New Testament are not mentioned. About two dozen prophets are named, most of them being characters from the Old Testament. Muhammad is the last and 'seal of the prophets', superior to all and superseding all.

The orthodox belief is that prophets are free from sin, though interestingly enough, Jesus is the only prophet of whom neither the Quran nor the Traditions mention that

He ever asked forgiveness of God. Of the sinlessness of
Jesus no orthodox Muslim has any doubt. In this respect
He is superior to Muhammad. The chief passages in the
Quran referring to our Lord state that He was born of the
Virgin Mary, that He spoke in His cradle to vindicate the
chastity of His mother, that He performed miracles, and
that He was not crucified. The fundamental reason why
Muhammad denied the crucifixion was that he could not
conceive of an apostle of God being treated so
ignominiously.

No particular importance has been attached by Muslims
to the actual birth, life and death of their Founder. In
Islam revelation was not in Muhammad but in the message
disclosed to him and gathered by him in a book, the Quran.
It has always been what he taught as revealed truth that
matters because he is thought to be the instrument of
revelation, not the incarnation of God and redeemer of the
world. In the Christian religion, on the other hand, it is
not so much what Jesus said as what He was and is and did
that makes Him the unique disclosure of God, entirely
different from all other religious founders, prophets,
teachers and mystics. "God, having of old time spoken
unto the fathers in the prophets by divers portions and in
divers manners, hath at the end of these days spoken unto
us in His Son, Whom He appointed heir of all things"
(Heb. i. 1f.).

Since Muhammad founded a religion, he cannot be
judged like any other 'strong man', say, of the Napoleonic
type. He must submit to be judged by ethical and religious
standards. The comparison between Muhammad and Jesus
must inevitably present itself. Since Islam claims to be a
universal religion, and even to supersede Christianity, Muslims themselves must submit to having their Prophet judged
by the highest moral and religious standards known to men.

But Muslims are usually extremely sensitive to any criticism of Muhammad, maintaining that such criticism is irrelevant since the Quran was not of his own devising. If once
they admit a human as well as a divine element in the
Quran, they will be driven anew to study Muhammad; and
here it is difficult to see how, on any impartial estimate of
history, the fiction that Muhammad was 'innocent, simple-
minded, truthful and sweet-tempered' can then be maintained.

Influenced probably by the Christian reverence for Jesus,
Muslims have elevated Muhammad to the position of the
ideal man and have made religion to be the imitation of
him. He himself stated that his function was to be a mes-
senger of God to man; he was a man among men and had
no power to work signs and miracles. But popular Islam
has not taken Muhammad at his word, and has turned him,
despite contrary evidence, into a miracle worker and into
the perfect man who committed no sin. Supernatural gifts
have been attributed to him. "He could see in front, also
behind and in the dark; did he walk with one who was
taller than he, he equalled him in height; sitting down
his shoulders were above those who sat with him; his body
threw no shadow because he was all light". He was the
model of manly beauty, the highest morality, the centre and
pivot without whom there can be no religion.

The Ibadhis, who are represented in Zanzibar, reject
this extreme form of veneration, but its influence is apparent in the uncritical acceptance of the superiority of
Muhammad by the majority of East African Muslims[1].
After the death of Muhammad the traditions about his life
began to be manufactured. In those days it was no sin to

[1] In Zanzibar, for instance, one of the most popular books is
called Maulid Barzanji, and contains religious verses in exaggerated praise of the Prophet read on the celebration of his
birthday in both private houses and mosques.

put into a man's mouth words that he might have said or
to polish and embellish what he actually had said. One,
who believed firmly that he obeyed the prophet, had no
hesitation in ascribing his ideas to Muhammad; if he had
not said these things, well, he ought to have done. Although
the Traditions have been classified with numerous sub-
divisions, sound, respectable and weak, African Muslims
know very little about their fabrication and cannot be
expected to examine them for their authenticity.

*　　　　*　　　　*

The Traditions, *hadith,* are details concerning the figure
of Muhammad, whereas the Custom, *sunna,* is the resulting
whole, the habit of life which pious Muslims try to make
their own. The *sunna* is enshrined in the *hadith* and the two
words are sometimes used interchangeably, but properly
there is a difference between them. Those who profess to
follow the *sunna* call themselves Sunnis, as distinct from the
Shi'as, the party of 'Ali, cousin and son-in-law of Muhammad.' The majority of Arab-Swahili Muslims are Sunnis,
and the Shi'as are represented only by Indian communities.
Most tribal African Muslims follow Arab-Swahili leader-
ship, though it is highly doubtful whether, if some were
asked individually if they were Sunnis, they would understand what was meant. The word *sunna* is not used in the
Swahili language and the word *hadithi,* meaning a story or
tale, is used with no special religious connotation. It would
be wrong to presume from this that African Muslims are
ignorant of the Traditions, for the Sunna is taught in the
mosques, but it does show that Africans do not think of
themselves as Sunnis[1]. They do not understand the difference

---

[1]They may know that they are not Shi'as, but without understanding the difference.

between the Sunnis and the Shi'as, nor the origins of the Traditions. Not infrequently they wrongly attribute to the Quran what really belongs to the Traditions. There is no clear appreciation of the Traditions as a separate source, second in authority only to the Quran itself.

*   *   *

5. . . . . and in the Resurrection and the Last Day.

Muslims are taught to believe that the actions of men will be weighed in the balance and judged accordingly. Intercession for Muslims will not avail, though Muslims, after being purged, will enter Paradise. Great merit is attached to the intercession of Muhammad. Details of heaven and hell are mentioned by commentators, some reasonable and some fantastic.

Bodily resurrection is clearly taught in the Quran. A constant, popular feature in the representations of judgment, frequently mentioned in Swahili religious verse, is the 'Bridge' (Arab. *sirat*). This is stretched over hell and is finer than a hair. In their attempts to cross it the wicked will fall into the fire beneath. The righteous will pass over with the speed of lightning.

A sign of the last day is the second advent of Christ. For Muslims, as well as for Christians, the Messiah is Jesus, Who, according to orthodox Muslim belief, did not die, but was taken up alive into heaven, whence He will come again to kill Dajjal, or Anti-Christ, to destroy churches and crosses, and to kill those Christians who do not believe in Him as true Muslims should. Associated with this belief is belief in the Mahdi, a word meaning 'guided', referring in this context to one who stands in a specially close relation to God. The Mahdi is the ruler who will restore all things and usher in the golden age. Jesus will help the Mahdi to re-establish the Muslim faith.

The Sunnis have never regarded the Mahdi as specially important, but only as one of the figures who will herald the end of the world. For the Indian Shi'as, however, the idea of the Expected One, referring to a hidden imam or leader who will return to rule in righteousness, is common in all their sects. For the Africans, there would be no need even to mention this belief in the Mahdi, because, as we have said, most Africans are Sunnis, and do not even know of this belief. But a minority of African Muslims belong to the Ahmadiyya sect, whose leader, Mirza Ghulam Ahmad Khan of Qadian in the Punjab, claimed to be both Messiah and Mahdi, asserting that his coming was foretold in the Old Testament, the New and the Quran.

Ghulam Ahmad (1839-1908) realized that it would substantiate his own claim to be the Messiah if it could be proved that Jesus had died and been buried, and that that was the end of His career so far as this world's destinies are concerned. Ghulam produced the 'proof'. He taught that Jesus was indeed nailed to the cross, but that He did not die thereon; He only swooned. After three days He revived, and was so far restored by a marvellous ointment—'the ointment of Jesus'—that He was able to undertake a mission to the lost ten tribes of Israel, who, he maintained, were dwelling in Afghanistan and Kashmir. Finally He died a natural death in Srinagar, where Ghulam 'discovered' His tomb.

The Ahmadiyyas now claim to number some half-a-million, in more than a dozen countries, and one branch of them has established a mosque in South London. Even though they are regarded by the orthodox as heretics, they are more able defenders of their faith than any of their contemporaries. There are no more active propagandists in the Muslim world to-day; it is significant that of all the

Indian Muslim sects, this is the only one to establish itself amongst tribal African Muslims.

The Ahmadiyyas are responsible for the new translation of the Quran into the Swahili language. They are conservative in their attitude to the Quran, claiming to interpret that book in the light of present-day conditions. In doing so, they are quite ready to besmirch the character of Jesus by charging Him with cowardice, drunkenness, disrespect to His Mother, friendliness with women of ill-repute, and blasphemy. This is somehing which no orthodox Muslim would feel free to do. They attack the Bible by quoting freely from articles by radical critics. They appeal to all Muslims for funds, claiming that Ghulam Ahmad is the latest renewer of religion, one of whom is expected every hundred years.

While it is possible to indicate the obviously heretical nature of the Ahmadiyya sect, the sect cannot be judged entirely by reference to the beliefs associated with it. There was a split in the sect in India, and the seceders aimed at minimizing the differences between themselves and other Muslims. The Ahmadiyya in East Africa belong to this more moderate group, and they make no attempt to emphasize the claims of their leader, Ghulam Ahmad.

For this reason, to the tribal African the sect appears orthodox enough, and no doubt most of its African adherents would be greatly surprised to know the truth about its founder. They do not regard themselves as different in any way from other Muslims, and perhaps, from the Muslim point of view, it is just as well that they should not know too much about the difference. The unorthodox Muslim will not go out of his way to point out the difference, for what is the point of disturbing the minds of those who are accepted as Muslims? As it is written,[1] "The

[1] Quoted by Tritton, ibid.

heart free from uncertainty is a better Muslim than a breast
stuffed with doubt".

*   *   *

6. . . . . and in the Predestination of Good and Evil.

Fatalism is the ruling principle in the thought and life of
every Muslim. *Inshallah,* 'if God will', is always on the lips
of the African believers. Allah's will explains and accounts
for everything that happens. All that has been and all that
will be was decreed in eternity and was written on the
Preserved Tablet, which contains the heavenly Quran, the
prototype of that in the hands of men, and the record of
all that is and is to be.

The emphasis in the Quran is undoubtedly fatalistic, but
there are many passages which stress the personal responsibility of accepting God's message and the value of righteous
living with its reward. Muhammad was essentially a
preacher, whose message (and its emphasis) was adapted
to the needs of the occasion. His aim was to gain converts,
not to present a well-balanced dogma. It took about three
hundred years for a dogma to be worked out by the
theologians, and this can be described as the dogma of
camouflaged fatalism. It meant retaining God as the
Absolute, with power to will and to do evil, but God who
allows man certain powers. It meant that if God wills a
thing, He creates in man the power to do it. The doing of
the thing willed by God is the act of man, establishing
his personal responsibility. By this the absolute will of God
is accepted as imperative whatever is done by man or not.
The Muslim is on the safe side any way, because God has
willed for him to be born a Muslim.

In practice fatalism does not mean leaving everything to
God, but it does mean for the Muslim an attitude of

indifference over the outcome. For many, of course, this results in inactivity, but this side of fatalism has perhaps been over-emphasized by Christian observers. There is another important factor resulting, namely, that the Muslim accepts adversity and misfortune without undue regret, for what has been is God's will. A Muslim submits and thereby saves himself much nervous worry and exhaustion.

This attitude prevents the Muslim from feeling guilt or remorse. In the Christian religion contrition, sorrow for sin, is of basic importance, providing the foundation for building a new and better life. Sin in Islam is simply that which Allah forbids. There are certain things permitted *(halal)* and others forbidden *(haram)*. Just as in the early days of Islam, the idea of things forbidden *(haram)* for tribal African Muslims is that of taboo.

In higher levels of Islamic society the distinction between *haram* and *halal* is that between what is unlawful and what is lawful, and need not be too closely identified with any system of ritualistic taboo, but the tribal African Muslim is familiar with such a system and must certainly be influenced by it in his life as a Muslim. Every African tribe has a very long list of actions which are taboo, it may be taboo to meet a chameleon on a path, for women to eat eggs, etc., etc., actions harmless enough in themselves, but which, because they are declared taboo, must be avoided. There are ceremonial ways of putting the matter right if such actions are unwittingly performed.

There is nothing in Islam which resembles the Christian conception of sin as a fall from grace, an alienation from God. In the absence of any feeling of estrangement between God and man, there is no need for reconciliation, no need for redemption, nor for a Saviour from sin, nor for being born again in the likeness of the Spirit. This reveals the great gulf separating Christianity from Islam.

The unpardonable sin in Islam is to conceive another
god besides God. The Christian doctrine of the Trinity is
interpreted by Muslims as an abominable offence against
the unity of God. Muhammad himself seems to have had
the idea that Christians believed in three gods, God the
Father, God the Son and Mary, the Mother of God.
Christians, of course, repudiate this false concept of the
Trinity, but Muslims do not accept the Christian doctrine,
and therefore regard any Christian, however good or holy
he may be, as perpetually committing the unpardonable
sin of destroying the unity of God.

Chapter Six

MUSLIM LAW AND PRACTICE

African Christians on the mainland dioceses of the Universities' Mission in East Africa have always looked to Zanzibar as the cradle of their Church, and quite rightly so. The Church in East Africa developed from the island. Zanzibar is still in the religious sense the cultural home of the mainland Christians, even though most of them may have never been there. The influence of African priests trained in Zanzibar by men like Bishop Weston is apparent in the life and form of the Church on the mainland.

What of the mainland Muslims? Do they look to Zanzibar as their cultural home in the religious sense? Peculiarly enough, they do not. While the personal influence of His Highness Seyyid Khalifa, Sultan of Zanzibar since 1911, has had an altogether beneficial effect in maintaining, by his own example of strict religious observance and never-failing tolerance, a stable Muslim community both in Zanzibar and on the mainland, the mainland Muslims do not belong to the same religious sect as their acknowledged head, the Sultan. It has already been noted that the majority of mainland African Muslims are orthodox Sunnis; the Sultan of Zanzibar is of the unorthodox Ibadhi sect.

The influence of the Sultan in the general Islamic community, however, is much greater than the influence of the Ibadhi sect. In the world of Islam and in East Africa in particular, the influence of the Ibadhis is negligible. It is a very old sect, the last remnant of the Kharijites, a political group who separated very early in Islamic history. To-day they are found as a community only in Oman off the South

Arabian coast, in Zanzibar and in Algeria. They are a
people with characteristics not to be found elsewhere in
Arabia.

Dr. P. W. Harrison in his book, *The Arab at Home,* has
written as follows about the people of Oman, the Sultan's
original home: [1]

"Religiously they are earnest and faithful in all
observances of their own faith; none indeed are more so,
but they are tolerant and open-minded to a degree unknown
elsewhere in Arabia. Religious discussions are not taboo in
that country, and I have even had men ask for a Christian
service so that they might come and see what it was like".

The Sultan's kindly tolerance would seem therefore to be
in the tradition of his birthplace, and this may explain why
he has never used his exalted position to force his own form
of religion upon his people. He has always been the first to
extend cordial support to every kind of religious enterprise,
whether by Christians, Hindus or by Muslims of whatever
sect.

And yet the Ibadhis consider themselves the only true
Muslims. They are extreme literalists in their interpretation
of the Quran. Women have a greatly honoured place in
their social and religious life, a fact worth noting in view
of the inferior position allotted to women by many orthodox
Muslims on the East African mainland. In Oman itself,
the women have their own mosques, and there is, according
to Dr. Harrison, a surprising degree of comradeship in
married life amongst the Ibadhis compared with other parts
of Arabia.

*   *   *

Since the tenets of the Ibadhi sect have not been purpose-
fully offered to the majority of the Sultan's people, how
does it come about that they are what they are, orthodox

[1] Harrison, P. W., p. 100.

Sunnis? The reason is that the majority of Arabian sailors and merchants who married African women and who in fact established the Swahili race were themselves orthodox Sunnis. They came especially from the Hadramaut and from the coastal districts of the Persian Gulf. Wherever these early traders settled they established small colonies in small stone-built citadels or cities of their own construction. Someone of the camp-followers who was qualified was appointed as an *imam* of the mosque, and placed in charge of the instruction of converts. The mosque was the central building of the settlement, generously and skilfully built. The ruins at Kilwa, Songo Manara, Gedi and other places along the coast are examples of the early Muslim citadels.

The Sunnis, orthodox followers of the *sunna,* or custom, of the Prophet, are divided into four schools of jurisprudence. These schools of law are not sects, for a man may transfer his allegiance from one to another without being guilty of schism. Most African Sunnis belong to the Shafi'ite school.

* * *

The intimate connection between law and religion in Islam is very great. While the conception of Muslim law may often be very hazily conceived and imperfectly understood, yet it wields a powerful influence over the minds of the majority of African Muslims in the villages, and reverence for it is maintained to the best of their ability.

The technical term for the law of Islam is *sharia*. It extends to every detail of the private and domestic, social and political relationships, and the religious duties of the believer. It affects the African Muslim most intimately in matters concerning marriage and inheritance. Kadhi Ali bin

Hemedi El-Buhriy of Tanga has written much on the subject in the Swahili language. Commentaries have been
written by hand in Swahili on the leaves of Islamic law
books in Arabic. The subject is of great scope, and one can
do no more here than just mention a few points of interest.

*   *   *

The legal background of Islam may be foreign to African
traditional society. This is especially the case amongst the
matrilineal tribes of East Africa, which have a different
system of family and clan relationship from that associated
either with Islamic or with Christian society. The members
of a matrilineal tribe cannot all become Christians without
fundamentally disturbing the traditional system of kinship.
The same is true for conversion to Islam except that Islam
allows for polygamy. African tribes have been known to
change from being a matrilineal society to a patrilineal one,
but with polygamy retained; this has occurred where neither
Islam nor Christianity has caused the change. The mainten-
ance of polygamy makes the change easier for Muslims
than for Christians, but a change is nevertheless inevitable.

Islamic law is not then to be identified with traditional
African law; polygamy is not practised for the same reasons
nor under the same circumstances under both systems. In
Islam marriage legislation limits the number of legal wives
to four, with the condition attached that the husband must
deal equitably with them, otherwise he should take only
one wife. In Arabia this put a restriction upon the Arab
who usually had more wives than four. The dowry system
gave the wife an independence inasmuch as she became
the sole owner of a considerable part of the dowry.

Any reference to polygamy must include the fact that in
East Africa polygamy is not practised on anything like so

large a scale as it is, say, in West Africa. Most polygamists in East Africa have two wives and many African pagans have only one. While it is true that to become a Christian an African must discard all his wives but one, there are many Africans who need not make this arrangement, because they have only one wife at the time of their conversion. Pagan monogamy is common enough in Tanganyika. It is no special attraction to such men to know that in Islam they may take more than one wife. That is possible for them in pagan society, but they may not be able to afford a second wife in any case.

Even the permission for polygamy is strongly opposed by the Christian Church. Whether in Islam or in tribal African society, polygamy puts women at a great disadvantage. One factor which accentuates their inferiority in Islam, and indeed makes family life in Islam generally unstable, is that divorce is the sole right of the man, a right which he can exercise at his pleasure without giving the least explanation. On the other hand, if the wife has given birth to a son, her position is fairly well ensured in the family.

*   *   *

The strict interpretation of the Quranic law in its full range is not expected of the African Muslim. In family matters even, he may prefer the customary African law. It depends upon the strength of customary tribal life, and this can still be very strong indeed in the rural areas. But Muslim law is flexible and accommodates itself to the traditional rules of African society. There is no religious autocracy to compel African Muslims to follow the Quranic law, so that whether they do or not is seldom a matter of serious conflict. In the established Muslim communities on the coast, of course, Islamic law is taken for granted and willingly accepted.

Muhammad brought laws, often going into great detail. Christ laid down principles upon which true life is based and can grow. The unwritten laws of African tribal society which are implicit in custom are often as detailed as Islamic laws. The popular western idea of 'the law of the jungle', meaning usually the absence of any authority at all, is altogether false in relation to customary African law. Pagan Africans were never at liberty to do what they like, but were bound by a highly complex system of conduct in the fulfilment of which the individual lost his personal freedom of action. He had to follow tribal custom or pay the penalty of physical punishment or social ostracism. With the break-down of tribalism the sanctions which helped to enforce customary law have been drastically weakened, and Africans are forced to look for a new guide for conduct. They hold fast to customary law for as long as they may, often observing a measure of both customary and Islamic law.

Many Africans find in Islamic law a satisfactory substitute for their customary law, not least because it goes into such great detail concerning matters about which customary law was equally detailed. Africans are so used to having all individual action ruled by custom and precedent, that many welcome a religion which lays down the law in the minutest particular. Immature Christian converts do not understand an attitude which 'counsels' certain lines of conduct, or 'deplores' others, but fails to lay down the law. It will take several generations to create the atmosphere in which true Christian liberty can be exercised.

*   *   *

Christian liberty is expressed on many various levels of individual conduct and this has resulted in a rich variety of

Spirit-led human action. But Islamic law tends to keep Muslims on the same level of conduct. There is a sameness about Muslims who fulfil the Quranic law. The same can be said of Christian converts wherever the 'Thou shalt not' attitude has been over-emphasized by the missionary. This negative attitude was perhaps necessary in the early days when Africans had to be introduced for the first time to the Christian moral law, but in doing so the law of liberty was almost excluded from instruction to converts. It may be held that they were not ready for it; some missionaries would maintain that most Africans are not yet ready. But they must be given the chance of being made free by much greater emphasis upon the positive aspects of freedom from the law by response to God's grace.

Muslims are bound by their own laws, because they have no doctrine of grace. The resulting uniformity of conduct keeps the great majority of Muslims on the same human level. But the purpose of religion is to raise man from his human level to a higher level, to the divine level. Christianity sets before man a goal which he cannot attain by his own efforts alone. He must bring himself into contact with the divine power and live in the strength of that power. There must be spiritual tension if he is to live the Christian life.

There is no such tension in Islam. Consequently, Islam becomes just an ethical system, and its believers become formalists for whom the outward practice of religion is the means of gaining favour or merit with God. Every religion tries to guard against formalism, and Islam is not exceptional in this respect; the believer is expected to make an intention before he prays. But in practice, the emphasis in Islam upon the manner of prayer, its ritual form, usually results in an exclusively formalist approach. The absence of spiritual tension in prayer, combined with this over-emphasis on prayer-ritual, keeps the believer on the lower, formal level of prayer.

Even so, this emphasis upon outward religious practice results also in a corporate spirit. Muslims are bound more closely together by the performance of their religious duties. We know that fellowship vitalizes prayer, but it is equally true that communal prayer vitalizes the fellowship. We should not underestimate the value of the performance of a form of worship which has to be dutifully performed. It is sometimes maintained that Africans prefer a religion with ritual. If this be true in relation to the ritual of the Catholic Church, and there is much to be said for this point of view, then it is equally true in relation to Islam. For prayer itself in Islam is a ritual; the greater emphasis on this ritual for Muslims increases the danger of the ritual becoming not a means to an end, but the end itself.

*   *   *

The practical duties of the Muslim are summed up under the term *din*, an Arab word from the same root as the Hebrew *din*, 'to judge', and as a borrowing in Swahili the word *dini* means 'religion'. The five principal duties are said to be obligatory, because they are based directly on the Quran. These five duties, often called the five pillars of Islam, are (1) Recital of the Confession of Faith, (2) Recital of Prayers, (3) Fasting, (4) Almsgiving, and (5) Making the Pilgrimage to Mecca.

Canon Dale in his book *Islam and Africa*[1] omits the first of these duties and includes as the fifth duty the Holy War, but although in Islamic history an attempt was made to add a sixth duty, namely the Holy War, it was never included as one of the five duties obligatory for a Muslim. The

[1] Dale, ibid. p. 95 et seq.

Wahabbis, who are represented by a minority of Muscat Arabs in Zanzibar and in a few other places along the East African coast, are followers of a sect founded by an Arab who called for religious war, but the members of this sect in East Africa in no way emphasize this aspect of their founder's teaching. The wonderful daggers worn by these men as they walk in stately fashion through the narrow streets of Zanzibar are highly decorative, but, sharp as they may be, are fortunately not the weapons of religious warfare.

To omit the first of the practical duties, the Recital of the Kalima, or Confession of Faith, is to omit what for many mainland African Muslims may be the most important of all. At least this is the one duty which they all can fulfil as adequately as the most devout and well-instructed Arab from the Hadramaut. As for the other four duties, it is difficult to estimate the extent to which mainland African Muslims fulfil them. It depends very much upon the strength of the Islamic community in any tribal area and also upon established tradition. Amongst the Yaos of Southern Tanganyika (Masasi Diocese), for instance, there is quite a strong Islamic element and this is connected with the Islamic tradition of that branch of the Yao tribe further south in Nyasaland and Portuguese East Africa.

While it would be possible to give instances of tribal Africans who give trivial reasons for being Muslims, e.g. so that they might wear the conventional Muslim dress of a long white garment and a red fez, it should be granted that the majority of tribal African Muslims have at least the intention of practising their religious duties. This intention may not always be a purely religious one, for it may be prompted by thoughts of increased prestige. But then very much the same approach to their religion is made by some converts to the Christian religion and with greater reason, for Christianity offers the convert more than the consolations of religion. Many Africans are attracted to the Christian religion from non-religious motives, for what goes with the religion, western education and the opportunities of earning money which this education brings, and not always for the religion itself. The missionary's converts are often his greatest burden as well as his greatest joy.

It would be too much to expect African converts either to Islam or to Christianity to be at once mature in understanding and in belief. There are babes in Muhammad as well as 'babes in Christ'. From the point of view of the converting religion both are equally precious and deserving of careful nurture. The question is which religion provides, for its own purposes, the best crêche. It would be admitted by educated Muslims that under the conditions prevailing in the African tribal areas the advantage here, for the time being at any rate, is with Mother Church.

One has only to compare the average church with the average mosque in these tribal districts where both may be found. In most instances the church, humbly built as it may have been by the villagers themselves, is far superior to the miserable structure which serves as a mosque. The spirit which has prompted Muslims to build some of the noblest religious buildings in the east appears to be completely absent on the African mainland and even in many places along the coast. There is no attempt even to emulate the standard of religious-building set by their fellow Africans who are Christians. The reason may lie in the absence of any outside authority for the Muslim community.

The churches have been built by the African Christians, but most frequently by the initiative and under the direction of the white missionary or of African clergy trained by the missionary. Islam on the East African mainland has no corresponding authority from Arabia or from anywhere else. There is the Muslim teacher, but often he is just one of themselves. It is sometimes difficult enough for the white missionary to encourage his Christians to build and keep in repair the simplest village church, but because he is a white man, he usually gets it done. How much more difficult for the Muslim teacher, who may not even have the urge to do the same for the building of a better mosque.

For establishing an indigenous African Church, a Church of the people, the presence of an outside authority afforded by the white missionary is a temporary necessity. He introduces the people to a way of life which otherwise would not have been possible for them. The last missionary will leave only when the African Christian community is strong enough to maintain itself without any depreciation of Christian witness or religious strength. But for establishing Islam no such outside authority is deemed necessary. Although Islam is far more authoritarian that Christianity in the sense of prescribing the minutest detail of human conduct and religious behaviour, it is self-propagating. There is no priesthood in Islam, and for the Africans at least no religious leaders who give practical directions suitable to Muslims living in rural areas.

The consequence is that in contrast to the Christian Church on the East African mainland Islam seems, and in fact is, for the present a backward community. We may well ask what the Christian community would be like in East Africa if the missionaries were removed from it together with the western benefits which the missionaries bring. The resulting community of African Christians could then more fairly be compared with the Islamic community. Would the comparison be favourable to the Christians? We most earnestly hope so. Until we can be absolutely sure of this, even though of course such a situation could not now arise, it may be as well to suspend too hasty a judgment upon the Muslim villagers and their pathetic little mosques.

The indigenous nature of Islam on the East African mainland is then at once its weakness and its strength. Too far removed from the real world of Islam to be very effective, what feeble Islamic roots there are do at least go down into African soil.

*   *   *

Prayers are more meritorious if said in a mosque, but they may be recited in private. The face must be turned towards Mecca, and the direction is indicated in every mosque by a niche (*mihrab*) set in one of the walls. The prayer-leader (*imam*) turns in this direction, and the congregation, placed behind him, follow his movements exactly. Anyone can be the prayer-leader, but usually one person undertakes this office, which is the nearest approach in Islam to there being a minister. He is not a minister in the Christian sense. All men are equal in the mosque, and of this equality Muslim writers make frequent mention, though outside the mosque the equality of believers is only theoretical. Social distinctions are accepted as being the will of God.

The set times of prayer are: dawn, noon, mid-afternoon, sunset, and two hours after sunset. Before each time of prayer, the believer must perform certain ablutions meticulously according to fixed rules. The worshipper must be ritually clean, and without these ablutions prayer is void, even sinful. Some pollutions demand a bath, but otherwise, to fulfil the religious regulations, it is enough to wash the face, hands and feet with care, water must be sucked into the nostrils, the wet fingers put into the ears, and the hands passed over the hair. If water is lacking, sand or dust may be used.

The call to prayer in African mosques is made from the door, in the absence of a minaret. The prayers themselves must be said in Arabic, and consist mainly of passages from the Quran, interspersed with ejaculations and formulae ascribing greatness to God. The prayers are accompanied by postures prescribed with utmost detail, the violation of any of which nullifies the whole prayer. The first posture is standing, then bending forward with hands on knees, then prostrated with forehead touching the ground. To enable him to prostrate himself in this way the Muslim wears a brimless fez or cap, which he keeps on during the recital. The Arabic word for mosque is *masjid* which means the place of prostrating oneself before God. Each set of postures must be repeated as many times as are prescribed for each particular time of prayer.

The Friday prayer in the mosque has special merit. At mid-day special prayers are offered, and are preceded by a sermon (*khutba*) delivered by the *imam*. A great merit of mosque sermons is that they are always brief! It is reported that the prophet said: "Woe are ye when your sermons become long and your prayers brief". The sermons generally consist of exhortation to piety, and are in no sense the equivalent of sermons in Christian churches, though about this there might be some difference of opinion.

*　　　　*　　　　*

While the orthodox Sunnis use the term *imam* for the prayer-leader in the mosque or for the founders of the four schools of jurisprudence, the unorthodox Shi'as, who are predominantly Indian, use the term in referring to the Caliph (Ar. *khalifa*) or 'Successor' of the Prophet Muhammad. It was on the political issue of who was the rightful caliph that the Shi'a sects came into being. For the Shi'a's religion is the *imam*.

The most prominent section of the Shi'a in East Africa is that of the Ismaili Khojas, whose spiritual head is His Highness the Aga Khan, well known in Europe as a breeder of racing horses. To his Khoja followers in East Africa he is the forty-eighth Imam, the sinless and infallible successor of the Prophet. He has been one of the foremost leaders in Muslim reform movements and efforts to improve the condition of the Muslim community. It is very difficult to realize that this modern, cultured Indian prince is almost worshipped as an incarnation of deity by thousands of devotees, not only in East Africa but in India, in Iran and Central Asia, who pay him vast sums for the benefit of the whole community, and who count themselves fortunate if they ever have the opportunity to kiss his hand.

Most of the Khojas are Hindu converts or descendants of Hindu converts. They still follow the Hindu law of succession and Ismaili teaching has been adapted to the Hindus. This is not the place to discuss Ismaili belief in any detail, but it is sufficient to say that the emphasis upon the succession of the *Imam* affects their Islamic practice. For instance, at the daily prayers the pedigree of the *Imam*, from Ali the son-in-law of Muhammad through the seventh *Imam* Ismaili, is chanted as part of the service. The Khojas do not make the pilgrimage to Mecca, but those who are able go to the holy cities of Iraq, especially to the shrine of the martyr Husain at Kerbela, near the Euphrates.

Husain was the younger son of Ali, and when he and his company were betrayed and slain, most of those in whose veins the blood of the Prophet flowed thus perished. The descendants of the few who survived continued to be centres of fanatical devotion. The most spectacular of the Shi'a festivals is the mourning of Husain, which may be witnessed in Zanzibar during the first ten days of Muharram, the first month of the lunar year. During the day men parade the streets beating themselves with chains.

The organization of the Ismaili Khoja community centres round the Jama'at, or assembly in council of all adult males; there is no mosque, but community gatherings and daily religious services are held in the Jama'at Khan or council hall. The chief officials of every local community are the *mukhi* or treasurer, and the *kamaria* or accountant. Their main function is the collection of various customary contributions, the tithe as well as recurring dues, as on the festival of the new moon, and occasional dues, as on the rites of birth, marriage, burial, etc., all of which are forwarded to the Imam. Schools, clinics, libraries and dispensaries, as well as various charitable institutions are supported by this fund. When the Aga Khan was weighed in diamonds in 1946 and in platinum in 1953 all the money thus raised was given by His Highness into the central fund.

*   *   *

The most important Shi'a sect, but not as influential in East Africa as the Ismaili Khojas, is known as the **Ithnasharis** or The Twelvers (Ar. *ithna 'ashariyya*), and are so called because they believe that there have been twelve Imams. These can be termed the 'regular' Shi'as. Reformers in the Khoja sect of the Aga Khan have in the past seceded and joined the Twelvers. In 1927 a group of them addressed an 'Open Letter' to the Aga Khan and amongst the demands made on His Highness was the one "that you will change commercial Jama'at Khanas into mosques where prayer only might be offered".

Then there are the **Bohras** (or **Bohoras**) belonging to that branch of the sect in Gujarat who chose Daud B. Qutb Shah as their head. The word *Bohra*, said to be of Gujarati origin, and used not only by Muslims but by some Hindus as well, means a trader. For Hindus the word is a caste designation. The Bohra Muslims are mostly descendants of converted Hindus in the Bombay area. In Zanzibar a number of Bohras are ironmongers, tinsmiths, watchmakers and dealers in marine stores. The family of Karimjee Jivanji, a firm with estates of over 80,000 acres, is of this sect.

The Bohras keep themselves very much to themselves even in relation to the general Muslim community. The head of the Daudi branch, called the *mulla* or *da'i*, lives at Surat, and he is the supreme authority in religious and legal affairs. Their religious beliefs are very obscure, not least because a systematic practice of concealment obtains, and very little has been published. Although they do not normally associate with Hindus, they have clung to many Hindu customs. If a Hindu *dobi* or clothes-washer washes their clothes they purify them by sprinkling holy water on them. Yet they light illuminations on the Hindu festival of Diwali and begin new account books on that day.

The Daudi Bohras have their own exclusive mosques which they call Jama'at Khanas and their own cemeteries. Their calendar is two days ahead of the ordinary Muslim calendar. They offer only three prayers a day—morning, noon and night—instead of the usual five, and they do not meet on Fridays for united worship, as other Muslims do. They use the Gujarati language, with which they have mixed many Arabic words. They are said to pay one-fifth of their income to the *mulla* and further dues on births, marriages and funerals.

*   *   *

There are a few other sects, like the Maiman and the Sindhi, but the most important have been mentioned above.

They are all plainly marked with the stamp of their Indian origin. For the great majority of African Muslims, whether Arab-Swahilis or tribal Africans, these sects have very little practical significance. There is no purposeful modification of orthodox belief and practice by African Muslims. The intention is to be what their fellow African Muslims are, and that intention is made without choice or preference. They know very little about the sects. They are orthodox, but even that may not be understood. What matters is that they are Muslims.

So they try to copy what other African Muslims do, to pray and to fast. The fast for the whole of the month of Ramadhan is invariably observed. This means complete abstinence from any food or drink, including water, from smoking, or any other stimulant during the daytime; or, more exactly, from the moment a white thread can be distinguished from a black one in the early hours of the morning till sunset sharp. From sunset to that early morning hour, eating and drinking are permitted, and indeed Ramadhan often becomes a month of feasts by night. Africans in European employ often save up or ask for an advance in order to buy more rice during Ramadhan than they consume at any other time of the year. It is sometimes said that in the rural areas the fast does not involve any special discipline for Africans, because normally they have their first full meal of the day just before sunset. But it *is* a discipline, and especially in the case of the more educated few, who may be used to having meals or light snacks after the European fashion, it can be a very severe test of will and of religious devotion.

During the nights of Ramadhan the Quran may be chanted by special singers, religious poetry is intoned, and the *Dhikr* performed. The latter is a means of 'Remembering the Name of God'. Two rows of men stand facing each other and repeat the formula of faith, while swinging their bodies back and fore until they may reach a state of ecstasy or are exhausted. In some places women perform the *Dhikr*.

The practical result of Ramadhan is to knit the Muslim believers closely together. The individual is submerged in the common effort, and a spirit of elation and of fidelity to the community is often created.

Related to the subject of abstinence is the fact that Islam puts a ban on alcohol. In this respect Muslims are protected, to a certain degree, from what is one of the curses of rural Africa. Beer-drinking has an economic and social significance amongst rural Africans, and so long as it is practised temperately, the practice is altogether beneficial to the community. Only too often though, beer- and spirit-drinking becomes the occasion for drunkenness, even amongst Christians, and it is a problem serious enough to cause some missionaries to think that an outright ban on all forms of alcohol might profit the Christian community. In some parts of the Christian Church in East Africa, e.g. in the C.M.S. in Kenya, the ban is operative. In the U.M.C.A. dioceses, however, it is held that Christians should be taught to be temperate in a practice which, if accepted by genuine Christians, produced no harm but good. Apart from its economic and social justification, beer-drinking by rural Africans is an important item in their diet, possessing beneficial and necessary anti-scorbutic effect.

*   *   *

The two remaining duties obligatory for the orthodox Muslim are almsgiving and the pilgrimage to Mecca. For most tribal African Muslims these cannot be properly fulfilled. They have insufficient money to practise either duty in the normal manner.

Alms are of two kinds (a) *Zakat,* which is normally obligatory, and (b) *Sadaqa,* which is voluntary. The voluntary contribution is frequently made according to slender African means, but most rural Africans would by Muslim law be excused the payment of *Zakat* because they do not possess the minimum of property required to pay it. In most areas a small nominal sum is collected as *Zakat,* but it may bear no relation to the two and a half per cent levy on property which this tax normally entails. Assessment is difficult, and the tendency is for the payment to be left to the conscience of the individual. It is difficult to obtain reliable information on this matter. Generally speaking, in the rural areas there is no marked distinction between the two kinds of alms, but along the coast in the Arab-Swahili community the distinction is maintained. In the latter case the difficulty of assessment remains. Amongst the Indian Muslims, almsgiving is practised generously, but the purposes for which the money is used do not correspond with the orthodox use of *Zakat.*

The term Sadaqa, which means 'righteousness' is used in Swahili, as *Sadaka,* by the Christian Church, with the meaning of 'offerings,' or 'church dues' and it is interesting that without any suggestion of copying the dual kinds of alms from Islam, the Church also encourages members to give an annual sum for the spread of the Gospel, besides the normal offerings made Sunday by Sunday. The Sunday offerings are often made in kind, with eggs, maize, bananas, etc., but the annual sum is asked for in money. Although the annual sum is usually quite small, the fact is that African Christians in many areas do not pay it. They are so used to expecting everything to be done for them with European money, that it is difficult for them to understand the idea of self-support. Although according to western ideas the African is often a poor man, he is not so poor

as his Church offerings would suggest. He has to learn to
give and he could give much more than in fact he does. This
is an important matter for the future of the African
Church and missionaries take every opportunity of bringing home to the people their great responsibility in this
matter.

As for the pilgrimage, this obligation is subject to one
qualification, that the aspirant should be 'able to journey
thither'. For the great majority of African Muslims, this
must remain only a pious aspiration which will never be fulfilled. Along the coast, however, many African Muslims do
make the pilgrimage. Some save up over a period of many
years in order to go to Mecca. Boats are chartered and
leave every year for the holy city.

The pilgrim wears the prescribed garment of two white
cotton cloths, one wrapped round the loins and the other
thrown over the left shoulder. He must stand upon Mount
'Arafat, twelve miles from Mecca, on the ninth day of the
pilgrimage, go seven times round the Ka'ba, the leading
sanctuary, and kiss the meteoric Black Stone, which is
believed to be 'the right hand of God upon earth, stretched
out to his worshippers, even as a man gives his hand to
his brother'.

The concluding ceremony of the pilgrimage is 'the Feast
of Sacrifice', when the pilgrim sacrifices a sheep, or a goat,
or a cow, or a camel, according to his means, eats its flesh,
and distributes of it to those about him. This Feast of the
Sacrifice is simultaneously observed by Muslims all over
the world, and is one of the two yearly festivals kept by
Sunni Muslims, the other being the breaking of the Fast
of Ramadhan.

                    *   *   *

There can be little doubt that Islamic religious practice,

however partially fulfilled, gives to the Muslim believer a dignity which tribal African life does not always evoke. This dignity is highly prized by Muslims, who generally are fully conscious of it. They call it *heshima,* a word for which there is no exact English equivalent.

The tribal African notes the cleanliness, both in person and dress, of the Muslim and he appreciates the courtesy and good manners which express the quality of *heshima.* In Africa a man's *heshima* depends upon the esteem in which he is held in the public view. And this view, in a country where life is lived under public scrutiny, is a critical one. The Muslim therefore values *heshima* above all else, for it is the measure of his character and his life. It is not surprising that he should have his emulators from the villages of tribal African society.

Chapter Seven

MEETING THE CHALLENGE

In the Introduction to this book we quoted Dr. Samuel Johnson's dictum that all other religions except Christianity and Islam are 'barbarous'. The other religions of the world, like Hinduism and Confucianism certainly have one thing in common, that they know nothing of Christ. But Islam knows of Him.

The Quran teaches the Virgin Birth of our Lord, and the Traditions add the Immaculate Conception of His Mother. To Him alone of all the 'Prophets', including Muhammad himself, is imputed 'no sin'. Islam accepts His ability to work miracles and His flawless life, but it denies His Godhead, His Crucifixion and His Resurrection, and thereby rejects just those essential factors which make Jesus the Christ. Islam knows of Christ, but rejects Him.

This partial acceptance of Christ is reflected in the tendency to fixedness which characterizes Islam everywhere. It tends to raise the people up to its level, but to fix them there. It cuts off the possibility of further advance. The Muslim has just enough on which to rest and pride himself and no longer feels his own deficiencies, a certain amount of truth, a certain amount of civilization, a certain amount of toleration, but all these are so many obstacles to the acceptance of the fulness of Christ.

If Islam in East Africa were reformed of all abuses so that the religion was being practised free from any defect, it would still be utterly irreconcilable with the religion of the Cross.

*   *   *

The main issue of the Christian vocation is to be witnesses for Christ. In doing so before Muslims, it is important to remember that we are not introducing a new figure to their thinking. They think that they know Christ and that their knowledge of Him is more accurate than ours. A great deal depends then upon our right representation of our Lord. How can we best represent Him before Muslims?

In principle no difference of approach is necessary for mission work amongst Muslims than that which has always been adopted by the Universities' Mission amongst pagan Africans. A central characteristic of this work has been the self-identification, so far as is possible, of the missionary with African life and interests. By the simplicity and poverty of his life he has always been easily accessible to likely converts. And yet this self-identification, which follows the fundamental principle of the Incarnation of Christ Himself, cannot by the nature of things ever be complete. To the Africans the missionary, however closely they may live in contact with him, is always a foreigner.

Similarly, it is doubtful whether the western missionary can express the Christian message in such a way that it is relevant to the life of the Muslims whom he seeks to win for Christ. The idea of converting Muslims from within, by attempting to form groups of Muslims who have been converted and yet who maintain their social life within the general Muslim community, has been found impracticable. In what way then would it be possible for the missionary to identify himself with the Muslim community and yet to be fulfilling his mission? Certainly by living the Christ-like life, but conversions would not automatically follow.

He would be revered and respected, but he would remain a foreigner. This does not mean that such work would be profitless, but it would be restricted in its practical consequences. Very few conversions would result. As a religious principle self-identification with the people is of the greatest importance, but for the white missionary it remains only a religious principle and not a practical reality. This does not mean that the principle should not be acted upon, but that it needs to be supplemented by the indigenous witness of African Christians.

In the Netherlands East Indies the spread of Christianity amongst Muslims has been due to the witness of the native Church. The white missionary by himself could accomplish very little there. The same is true in any Muslim country where the Church exists. If Church life is weak in such areas, there is much less chance of gaining converts from Islam. Each convert has to be abstracted from the strong social medium of Islamic life, and there must be a strong religious and social community to which he can attach himself. This can be provided only by the native Church. The freedom of the Christian moral standard after the legalism of Islam is an insuperable problem to anyone living outside the Christian community. The convert from Islam cannot last long without open participation in Christian fellowship and public worship.

Religious change to Muslims is at bottom not change of belief but change of allegiance. This change is made more difficult in East Africa for Arab-Swahili Muslims because the native Church has its roots in tribal African society, a traditionally inferior society to the Arab-Swahili way of thinking. But it is for the indigenous church to remove this charge, often unfounded, of inferiority in cultural and social life. There can only be one effective way of doing this. Not by exclusive emphasis upon the benefits of western materialism, but by a better witness to the full power of Christ's Person and Life.

The missionary group to Muslims need not be westerners, but before they seek to change the allegiance of likely converts they must be absolutely convinced that the Christian society which is to receive them is such as will provide them with a true spiritual home. Although the change involves a break with the Muslim's religious past, it ought not to involve a break from the life that is natural to him if the Church into which he is received is truly indigenous. In the case of tribal African Muslims the change of allegiance is much easier than for Arab-Swahili Muslims, and certainly than for Indian Muslims.

The missionary aim, then, in East Africa must be to build the African Church to be a true spiritual home for converts. This is the work of the African Christian community, even more than of the white missionary. The fact that there is at present no white missionary of the Universities' Mission exclusively dedicated to the work of converting Muslims to Christ indicates, not only a lack of vocations for such work, but that the priority is still for strengthening the existing Christian community. The African Church is not yet strong enough to act itself as an efficient missionary force in relation to Islam; it has to be made so. All the help that the Mission can supply is at present devoted to maintaining the life of the existing Church. It is very much a younger Church, and needs to be fostered and guided if the labours of the past are not to be in vain. To neglect this work in favour of new work amongst Muslims would be to invite disaster.

But the challenge of Islam remains, and it is the knowledge of the thousands who know of Christ, but who do not accept Him, that should inspire supporters of the Mission, the missionaries themselves, and not least the East African Church of native believers to pray for spiritual power through our Lord Jesus Christ. This is what the African Church needs most, and by the prayers and practical support of friends in this country African Christians are helped to make their Church a real home, not only for themselves, but for Muslims who come to accept Christ as their Lord and their God. We cannot leave the conversion of Muslims entirely to the African Christians, but it cannot be achieved without them.

Our Lord prayed for all who should believe on Him through the centuries, and we may pray for the Muslims who by the power of the Word will in God's good time be brought into His Church:

"that they all may be one: as thou, Father, art in me, and I in thee, that they also may be one in us: that the world may believe that thou hast sent me".

SELECT BIBLIOGRAPHY

Arberry, A. J.	Islam To-day, 1943.
Arnold, T. W.	The Caliphate, 1924.
Arnold, T. W. and Guillaume, A.	The Legacy of Islam, 1931.
Brown, L. E.	The Prospects of Islam, 1944.
Cash, W. W.	The Expansion of Islam, 1928.
Cash, W. W.	Christendom and Islam, 1937.
Dale, G.	The Contrast between Christianity and Muhammadanism. Sixth edition, 1913.
Dale, G.	The Peoples of Zanzibar, 1920.
Dale, G.	Islam and Africa, 1925.
Donaldson, D. M.	The Shi'ite Religion, 1933.
Gairdner, W. H. T.	The Reproach of Islam, 1911.
Guillaume, A.	The Traditions of Islam, 1924.
Guillaume, A.	Islam, 1954. (Penguin Series).
Jones, L. B.	The People of the Mosque, 1932.
Macdonald, D. B.	The Religious Attitude and Life in Islam, 1909.
Margoliouth, D. S.	Mohammed, 1906.
Margoliouth, D. S.	Mohammedanism, n.d.
Mott, J. R. (ed.)	The Moslem World of To-day, 1925.
Rodwell, J. M.	The Koran (Everyman's Library).
Tisdall, W. St. C.	A Manual of Leading Muhammadan Objections to Christianity, 1915.
Tritton, A. S.	Islam, Belief and Practices, 1951.
Titus, M. T.	Indian Islam, 1930.
Walter, H. A.	The Ahmadiyya Movement, 1918.
Wensinck, A. J.	The Muslim Creed, 1932.
Zwemer, S. M.	The Moslem Christ, 1912.

INDEX